# DISRAELI

BORN: December 21, 1804
DIED: April 19, 1881

A man of great charm and persuasiveness, Benjamin Disraeli is best known for the role he played in the growth and development of England during the years of Queen Victoria's reign. As her Prime Minister, he instituted many domestic reforms in housing, public health and factory legislation, and because of his aggressive foreign policy England became one of the greatest colonial empires. Law student, newspaper publisher and a famous author at the age of twenty-one, Disraeli's consuming passion for politics led him from Parliament to Prime Minister of England, a post in which he served Queen and country till the day he died.

# Books by Manuel Komroff

DISRAELI

THOMAS JEFFERSON

NAPOLEON

MARCO POLO

JULIUS CAESAR

# DISRAELI

by
**Manuel Komroff**

Julian Messner, Inc.
New York

Published by Julian Messner, Inc.
8 West 40th Street, New York 18

Published simultaneously in Canada
by The Copp Clark Publishing Co. Limited

© Copyright 1963 by Manuel Komroff

Printed in the United States of America
Library of Congress Catalog Card No. 63–16787

# CONTENTS

# CONTENTS

# DISRAELI

# 1 A HOME IN ENGLAND

❖❖❖❖❖❖❖❖❖❖❖❖❖❖❖❖❖❖❖❖❖❖❖❖❖❖❖❖❖❖❖❖❖❖❖❖❖❖❖❖❖❖

BENJAMIN DISRAELI, ONE OF ENGLAND'S GREATEST prime ministers and beloved friend of Queen Victoria, was born in London on December 21, 1804. A new century had just been ushered in, a century which witnessed England's greatest glory. And Disraeli played the leading role in this shining moment of British history.

Disraeli loved England with full devotion; he dedicated his long life to the service and glory of England. And yet he never felt that he belonged to this land where he was born. Although both he and his parents had been born in England, Disraeli always felt like a stranger in his native country. He felt like an alien.

Why did Disraeli feel like this? He felt this way because from earliest childhood, when he first entered

9

grammar school, he was made aware of the fact that while he was like others, yet he was different, and this difference was very important. It set him apart from others, marking his personality and molding his character. Because of this difference he was unwanted, and many doors were closed to him. Because of this difference he was considered fair game for ridicule and abuse. This difference also presented him with problems which others were not called upon to face, problems which sometime seemed insurmountable. Yet step by step, with bold courage Disraeli conquered all difficulties and by force of character pried open all the doors which were closed to him.

What was it that set Benjamin Disraeli apart from others? What was it that made him different? It was his birth, his heritage. He was a Jew.

Benjamin Disraeli was an Englishman, but he belonged to a very old Spanish family of Jewish faith. Exactly when this family first settled in Spain nobody knows; however, its members seem to have lived there for centuries. It is possible that they came into the Iberian Peninsula shortly after A.D. 70 when the Romans burned down the Holy Temple in Jerusalem and brutally drove the Hebrews out of their ancient homeland, Palestine, to wander the earth seeking survival where they could—in Greece, Egypt, North Africa, India, China and what was then the barbarian forests of Europe.

Like all other Jewish families in Spain during the centuries of Moorish power, the Disraeli family seems to have grown and prospered. The Moors, who were Moslems, looked upon the Hebrews as first cousins both racially and religiously and always accepted them as equals. Under the joint rule of the Moors and Jews Spain rose to its greatest heights both socially and intellectually. Because of these two peoples Spain, during the Middle Ages, surpassed all the rest of Europe in medicine, science, mathematics, education, philosophy and —religious tolerance. Centuries later, after having left Spain, the Disraelis still glowed with the pride of their Spanish background.

But they did not forget their Hebrew origin and heritage. Their very name was a constant reminder to them of the noble past of their people. Disraeli has recorded that the family on arriving in Spain was so "grateful to the God of Jacob who had sustained them through unprecedented trials and guarded them through unheard-of perils" that they assumed the "name of Israeli, a name never borne before, or since, by any other family, in order that their race might be forever recognized."

Tolerance and progress blessed Spain during the time of the Moors, but as Moorish power gave way to Christian conquest the situation changed. With the coming of the Crusades, that passionate movement directed against the "infidel," the last vestiges of tolerance were swept away. Massacres of Jews and Moors began in Spain during the opening decades of the thirteenth century.

In 1278 a movement was launched to convert all Jews, and "black lists" were drawn up of those who refused to be baptized. In the fourteenth century the massacres increased. Whole towns were destroyed by fire and sword. In Valencia alone, 11,000 forced baptisms took place.

During the fifteenth century the massacres occurred at more frequent intervals. Waves of violence came every ten years until in the end the Inquisition was instituted; the State and the Church united to deal jointly and methodically with both the Jews and the Mohammedans. These heretics were to be rooted out at all cost. Courts were set up. Charges, mostly false, were made. Inhuman tortures were used to extract confessions of guilt. Property was confiscated; even the richest families were reduced to begging. Brutal prison terms were dealt out, and hundreds were burned at the stake. The terror mounted until it reached a climax in the year 1492. In this year all Jews, even those who had been converted, were expelled from Spain and their property real and personal was confiscated.

Leaving Spain the Israeli family went to Italy where it settled in the beautiful and rich seaport of Venice, which was then at the height of her glory. Two things only they took with them. Things which could not be confiscated. One was their pride as Spaniards and the other was their Hebrew heritage.

There in Venice, Disraeli has recorded:

Undisturbed and unmolested, my family flourished as merchants for more than two centuries under the protection of the lion of St. Mark, which was but just, as the patron saint of the Republic was himself a child of Israel. But toward the middle of the eighteenth century, the altered circumstances of England, favorable, as it was then supposed, to commerce and religious liberty, attracted the attention of my great-grandfather to this island, and he resolved that the youngest of his two sons, Benjamin, the "son of his right hand," should settle in a country where . . . public opinion appeared definitely adverse to persecution on matters of creed and conscience.

And so Disraeli's grandfather, Benjamin Israeli, left his home in Venice and went to England. He was eighteen years old. The year was 1748. His hopes for peace and freedom were high, and they were fulfilled in all ways but one—he found that in England, too, there was prejudice against the Jews.

It must be remembered that while the Magna Charta championed the rights of man and his personal liberties, England had a long history of persecution against the Jews. In 1210 King John I ordered all Jews imprisoned—men, women and children. To regain their freedom each one had to pay the crown a substantial ransom. In 1290, Edward I confiscated the property of all the 16,000 Jews in England and ordered them to leave the country at once, the land where they and their forefathers had lived for 200 years.

Other brutal persecutions of this nature continued for the next three centuries. And so even though the English eventually dropped such evil and unchristian ways, and even though Cromwell in 1655 had invited Jews to settle once more in England, traces of persecution still existed in 1748 in the form of outright prejudice. Jews were barred from Parliament, municipal offices and government services. They could not practice law nor were they admitted to any universities.

Benjamin Israeli brought with him to England his Spanish pride, his Hebrew heritage and an Italian accent. He was ambitious and energetic. He altered his name slightly to the more imposing D'Israeli.

"My grandfather," wrote Disraeli, "was a man of ardent character, sanguine, courageous, speculative and fortunate; with a temper which no disappointment could disturb and a brain full of resources." He became a merchant and small stockbroker. He entered into marriage with a wealthy Jewish girl whose dowry made him almost independent. He then became a member of the London Stock Exchange and bought a country house at Enfield not far from London. There he entertained friends, played whist and generally enjoyed life. His circumstances were enviable indeed, except for one thing, his wife Sarah, who was a very unhappy person.

Sarah D'Israeli had a brooding nature, and she deeply resented the fact that because of her Jewish faith she was not socially acceptable. She was descended from two very old and distinguished families. She was a member of the Spanish House of Xaprut, which had in the tenth century provided a vizier to the Caliphs of Cordova, and she was also directly related to the great Portuguese

House of Marrano of Villareal. Her pride of heritage was therefore strong. She felt that she was an aristocrat equal to any of the titled ladies of England. She reasoned that when England was still primitive her family was already rich, cultured and powerful. She writhed from the fact that she was a Jewess, and wanted to renounce her faith.

Bitterness took possession of her. She became very difficult and disagreeable. Her son and grandchildren have recorded that they remembered her only as one incapable of kindness. Because of these personality problems, she did irreparable damage to her only child, a boy named Isaac, who was born in the year 1766.

Mrs. D'Israeli found no pleasure in her son. Incapable of kindness she only criticized him. She was blind to all his virtues and tormented him without ceasing.

To escape from his mother, young Isaac turned to books and reveries. He protected himself with the armor plate of his imagination; his mother could not enter his world of fantasy. When he was only fourteen years old he wrote a long poem describing how he felt and what he saw in his secret world of make-believe.

Isaac's poem produced a family crisis. His father and mother were both seriously alarmed at the thought of having an only child who was a poet. They truly believed that all poets were doomed to live in poverty and squalor in dark garrets, continually in debt and hounded by the grocer, the baker and the milkman. And so steps were at once taken to correct this evil.

"The unhappy poet," records Disraeli, "was consigned like a bale of goods" to a business firm in Amsterdam. There the boy would learn the kind of poetry that businessmen write in ledgers. There he would learn about shipping, trade, invoices, bills, customs duties and everything else that the head of a large importing and exporting house must know.

But alas, Isaac was a born bookman. He lived with ideas. He felt ideas had values higher, much higher, than merchandise. Then too there was the temper of the time that could not be denied.

When Isaac landed in Holland the year was 1780. The American Revolution was near successful accomplishment. The venerable Benjamin Franklin was in Paris serving as America's first ambassador to the glamorous court of Marie Antoinette and Louis XVI. And throughout Europe the idea of liberty permeated the air. There was a twitch on the face of society that a few years later became a convulsion: the French Revolution.

So it is no great wonder that Isaac returned to England after four years of business training with little ledger knowledge. He had, however, accumulated another kind of knowledge. He had read Rousseau and become a disciple of this great political philosopher. He had also read deeply into Voltaire, whose works and ideas helped foster the French Revolution. And he had acquired a deep love for the language and history of his native England.

Isaac was now eighteen. His father suggested that to

complete his education he should go to France and work for another commercial firm. But Isaac now displayed a strong will of his own. He said, "No." And that "No" was final.

From that moment on his life was his own.

Isaac now devoted his time exclusively to his beloved books. Essays, poetry and fiction made up his entire existence. He read and wrote. And he went to Paris, where he formed a taste for book collecting and took great pleasure in exploring old libraries. Then returning to England, just before the outbreak of the French Revolution, he set to work to organize a great mass of notes and curious facts that he had collected.

Three years later this material was published in a volume entitled, *Curiosities of Literature*. This first work at once won him a position in the world of letters. He was only twenty-five. And this high position in literature he maintained to the last days of his life, producing many other notable works.

Byron thought highly of him and once said, "I don't know a living man's books I take up so often." Sir Walter Scott, who read his works with the greatest of interest, also held him in the highest esteem.

Reaching the age of thirty-six Isaac married the daughter of an Italian Jew. Her name was Maria, and unlike his mother, she was gentle, sweet-tempered and affectionate. She created for him a happy home very different from the stormy and bitter home of his youth.

Of this happy union four children were born. The eldest was a girl named Sarah. The second was a boy named Benjamin after his grandfather who had migrated to England from Venice. The two youngest were also boys. They were named Ralph and James. However, it was Benjamin, the second child of Maria and Isaac D'Israeli, who was destined to become world-famous.

While still an infant Benjamin was brought to the Spanish-Portuguese Synagogue by his parents and presented to God according to the ancient rites of the Hebrew faith.

Benjamin was from babyhood an unusual and lovable child. And as the months and years passed he grew to be a happy boy, noisy and spirited. He was his mother's darling and much favored by his father, who recorded that he had a quality which many boys did not possess, "He never lies."

Reaching the age of six Benjamin still possessed these qualities, but he now constituted a very serious problem to his parents. English boys of the middle and upper classes were usually sent to a private boarding school. However, Isaac D'Israeli, knowing how deeply rooted was the prejudice against Jews and what rude and tormenting treatment a Jewish boy would receive at Eton or Winchester, did not want to submit his son to such an ordeal. He was, therefore, forced to seek a private school which was smaller and more tolerant.

It was not an easy job which Isaac set himself, but at length, he felt that he had found the proper place, a school in Blackheath in southeast London. This school was run by a minister of liberal attitudes, and Isaac D'Israeli hoped that here his child would find tolerance and understanding. However, this did not turn out to be the case. His slender little son with his olive skin, dark eyes and dark curly hair looked very different from the other boys, who were mostly blond. He looked like a foreigner. So he suffered untold torture from the jibes of his schoolfellows, and he became the victim of several big boys, bullies who took pleasure in terrorizing him. He also suffered from the thoughtlessness of his masters. To give only one example, each evening, he was reminded that he was different and unwanted, for each evening the entire school, boys and masters, went to chapel for evening prayers, leaving him bewildered and alone.

It was a cruel and brutalizing experience. It seared his soul. He grew to hate school. "I was a most miserable child," he recorded. Yet he was courageous. He met his problems as best he could. Although he was very young and said he "hated field sports, indeed every bodily exertion," he took boxing lessons during his vacations so that he could protect himself against the boys who taunted him. In this way he substituted skill for brawn. And once roused to anger by an insult he would fling himself upon the bully and with fury beat him to a pulp.

Benjamin was very unhappy at school, but on week

ends when he went home, he knew true happiness. His family greeted him joyously, and he and his sister Sarah and his brothers and friends spent many happy hours together.

He loved to read adventure stories and biographies of great men. He dreamed that he too would someday be a great man, although in what field he would make his mark he did not know. He was a wonderful storyteller; he had a creative, imaginative mind. He told all kinds of exciting tales, and he invented wonderful games such as "Politics." It must be remembered that England was at that time at war with Napoleon and that politics was in the very air, and so Benjamin would gather Sarah and his brothers and friends around him and establish a "Parliament." They would make speeches, hold elections and enter into debates just like the members of the real English Parliament. Somehow Benjamin, who delivered the finest speeches and who knew just how to run things, was always chosen as prime minister.

Benjamin's parents knew that he was unhappy at school but they did not know what to do about it. However, beginning when he was twelve years old several very important changes occurred in his life.

His grandfather, Benjamin D'Israeli died, leaving Isaac D'Israeli his entire estate. It amounted to about $200,000, in our money, a great fortune in those days. Although Isaac and Maria D'Israeli had always been very comfortable, they were now rich, and they immediately moved to fashionable Bloomsbury Square, close to the British Museum and its wonderful library.

This pleasant change in circumstances, however, was almost immediately followed by a period of trouble which resulted in still another change in the family status, one which played the deciding role in Benjamin's future.

This very important change stemmed directly from a difficulty which arose between Isaac D'Israeli and his synagogue.

# 2 UNLOCKING THE DOOR

◆◆◆◆◆◆◆◆◆◆◆◆◆◆◆◆◆◆◆◆◆◆◆◆◆◆◆◆◆◆◆◆◆◆◆◆◆◆◆◆◆◆◆◆◆◆◆◆◆

ISAAC D'ISRAELI WAS A MAN WITH ORIGINAL IDEAS and an unfettered mind. He disliked all forms of theology and orthodoxy, and while he was perfectly satisfied with having been born Jewish, he never attended synagogue.

Now it happened that shortly after his father died, the synagogue appointed Isaac as one of its wardens. Being an honest and forthright person, Isaac immediately informed the elders that he could not accept the post. He explained that he felt there was a narrowness of outlook to all religious doctrines. Such a conviction, he continued, made him ineligible for a post which religious people, such as they, held in solemn awe.

The elders were shocked by Isaac's statement. After considerable deliberation and according to custom, they imposed a fine of forty pounds upon him.

Isaac refused to pay the fine. He, furthermore, proceeded to lecture the elders. As Disraeli later wrote, his father declared, "The inventions of the Talmudical doctors, incorporated in their ceremonies, had bound them hand and foot, and cast them into caverns . . . cutting them off from the great family of mankind. . . ."

After delivering strong words of defiance, Isaac asked to have his name struck from the membership roll of the synagogue. However, this request was refused because his fine still remained unpaid. And so the quarrel with the elders continued. It continued, in fact, several years or until Isaac, at length, gave in and paid the forty-pound fine.

Isaac was very happy to be free of orthodox ties. His nature and intellectual development did not require religion. He hoped that his children might grow up to feel as he did. But a friend who did not share his views now entered the scene. Using Isaac's own words, this friend said that Isaac had cut off his children from "the family of mankind" and that it was an act of cruelty to thus handicap young people who still had to make their way in the world. He went even further. He said that as members of the synagogue, Isaac's children were at a great disadvantage, but as members of the Church of England they would be freed of many prejudices. They would be eligible for all universities, and when they were grown they could enter law or politics if they chose. He recommended conversion.

Maria D'Israeli, who loved her children dearly and

naturally wanted to spare them from all unnecessary un-
happiness, sided with Isaac's friend. And so Isaac finally,
if reluctantly, consented to letting his children join the
Church of England.

In the months which followed, Benjamin read his
prayer books and studied his catechisms. Then, on July
31, 1817, he was baptized in St. Andrew's Church, in
Holborn, London.

Benjamin was thirteen years old at the time, and as he
stood beside the baptismal font and heard the words of
the solemn service he did not suspect what magical powers they possessed. Standing there that day, he did not
know that the words he heard were unlocking the doors
of Parliament and changing the course of English history.

With religious bars now removed, Isaac D'Israeli
wanted to take Benjamin out of the school at Blackheath
and send him to Eton and then to Oxford, but his wife
objected. She insisted that all "public schools," as private
schools are called in England, were places where boys of
Hebrew origin were unfairly treated. A compromise was
reached, and Benjamin was sent to a school not far from
London run by a Unitarian minister called Eli Cogan.

Although Benjamin also experienced prejudice in this
new school because of his foreign appearance and Jewish
parents, and although here too he was forced to fight
the bullies, the choice nevertheless proved to be fortu-

nate in some respects. Benjamin found the Reverend Cogan's school a most exciting and stimulating place—he describes it for us in one of his books:

> For the first time in my life I was surrounded by struggling and excited beings. Joy, hope, sorrow, ambition, craft, dulness, courage, cowardice, beneficence, awkwardness, grace, avarice, generosity, wealth, poverty, beauty, hideousness, tyranny, suffering, hypocrisy, tricks, love, hatred, energy, inertness, they were all there and sounded and moved and acted about me. Light laughs and bitter cries and deep imprecations, and the deeds of the friendly, the prodigal, and the tyrant, the exploits of the brave, the graceful, and the gay, and the flying words of native wit and the pompous sentences of acquired knowledge, how new, how exciting, how wonderful!

Benjamin's new school seems to have pleased him in many ways, yet his schoolwork did not interest him. The only subjects in which he excelled were speaking and writing. His schoolfellows were, in fact, so impressed by his use of language and his imaginative way of expressing himself that they soon looked up to him as something of a hero.

Benjamin naturally basked in the glow of this admiration, and to further his gains he organized a secret theatrical company, in direct violation of school rules. His parents had taken him to several plays, and so with unwarranted pride he felt he knew all that needed to be known about the theatre. He appointed himself director, stage manager and leading actor. The other boys were awarded supporting roles.

All went well at first, but after a few months this unequal division of honors led to jealousies. Feelings became more and more strained. Before Benjamin knew what had happened, he had been denounced by some of his actors to the Reverend Cogan. Then during play hour one of the boys hissed at Benjamin and said, "We have been led long enough by a foreigner."

All the pent-up emotions which Benjamin felt for being scorned because of his Jewish background welled up within him. He struck the boy in the face. A fist fight followed. Benjamin, who had been taking boxing lessons for many years, immediately had the upper hand, and his accuser was soon lying bleeding and senseless on the ground. The Reverend Cogan immediately summoned Mr. D'Israeli and asked him to remove his son from school.

Benjamin was fifteen when his schooling was thus brought to an abrupt end. He came home hating all schools, but being a determined and ambitious boy, he decided to educate himself. And his loving and indulgent parents consented.

His father's books and guidance were at his disposal. He needed no urging. He had a burning passion for knowledge. The whole house became his schoolroom. He carried armfuls of books and papers from one room to the other, studying first here and then there, a habit which distressed his father, who kept pleading, "Please keep your papers together."

Benjamin studied Latin and Greek and read widely and deeply in other fields. He studied the lives of great men, being very critical of those world leaders who looked "upon their fellow creatures as mere tools" to be used for their own aggrandizement.

Besides biographies he read history. But what he liked best of all was to read about politics. The moment he discovered that there was an "art of politics" he felt that "everything was solved." That indefinable emptiness in his nature he felt was at last supplied.

Politics now filled his mind. Politics took possession of him. He became positively intoxicated with politics. He recorded, "I paced my chamber in an agitated spirit, and panted for the Senate." In fact he already pictured himself addressing Parliament and rousing the whole house with his eloquence.

Isaac D'Israeli watched his son with keen interest but he was careful never to interfere. He had not forgotten those difficult days of his youth when his father and mother had tried to fashion him into a businessman. He left Benjamin alone to pursue his heart's desire.

However, at the end of two years, when Benjamin was seventeen, he announced that politics would be his career, his father suggested that perhaps his road would be easier if he first became a lawyer. Law was the one field in which all politicians were involved.

Benjamin agreed; he would study law. His father immediately arranged for him to serve in a well-known London law firm. In those days in England one studied the law by working directly under practicing lawyers and reading certain prescribed works on jurisprudence. After several years of such study and after passing examinations drawn up by an impartial board of lawyers, one received a certificate and was "called to the bar."

Benjamin served as private secretary to the most active partner in the law firm to which he was apprenticed. He took dictation, wrote letters, recorded interviews with clients and helped with the presentation of cases in court.

He observed, he listened, he measured and he weighed the situations and the men with whom he came in contact. Nothing escaped the keenness of his observation. Even though he was not yet eighteen, he became at this time, as he later observed of himself, "a cunning reader of human hearts."

The days Benjamin spent studying law were stimulating and rewarding, yet his thoughts were constantly centered on his dream of entering politics. When he had finished at the office for the day he would spend hours studying the orations of Cicero, Demosthenes, Caesar and other famous men who had possessed the gift of eloquence. While at the law office he faced the world of reality, at home, in the privacy of his room, he lived in another world, the world of his desires. He dreamed of becoming a great statesman. This was at the root of all his wishes.

Benjamin was impatient to enter politics and prove

himself, and the waiting was very hard. He knew that Byron was famous at twenty-five and that Pitt had become prime minister when he was only twenty-three. But Isaac D'Israeli considered his impatience a weakness of youth, and in his gentle way he would caution him, "Do not try to be a great man in a hurry."

Benjamin spent many long hours at the study of law and at his program of self-education, which while now curtailed had not been abandoned. He also worked at a new interest; he wrote some short articles for London newspapers.

It was at this period, when his name first appeared in print, that he dropped the apostrophe. "It looks too foreign," he remarked. "Spell it simply Disraeli." His sister Sarah and his two brothers also adopted this spelling, but his father retained the old spelling, by which he was known in literary circles.

Benjamin was busy with his work, but he somehow managed to find time for fun. He was a very sociable person and liked to go out with his friends and to join in the conversation at his father's table, where many of the most distinguished men of the day gathered.

Young Disraeli was rather conceited, almost brash, and would defend his point of view with even the most elderly gentlemen. His manner of dress was also disturbing. He did not have his dark curly hair cut as short as other men and instead of wearing suits made of worsted as was the custom, he wore black velvet suits with ruffles at the cuffs and black stockings with red clocks.

Such affectations, bordering on vulgarity, naturally jarred many people. Still he never failed to make himself liked. Hearing him speak people soon forgave and then forgot his conceit and dandified appearance. His keenness of intellect, wit, enthusiasm and charming manners quickly dispelled whatever reservations they may have had. This was particularly true of the ladies, with whom he was a great favorite. He was never shy in their company, and he knew how to compliment them most graciously.

Benjamin's dreams and ambitions drove him relentlessly on. For three years he worked without rest and with such intensity that during his twentieth year his health began to suffer. He complained of giddiness. The world seemed to spin around his head. His father, in his usual wise and loving way, proposed that they set out, together with one of Benjamin's friends, William Meredith, on a six-week tour of Belgium and the Rhineland.

The tour began with the cities of Belgium. The older man and the two youths walked miles and miles of city streets, visiting cathedrals, churches, universities and museums. Benjamin's letters home to his sister, Sarah, were filled with details.

At Ghent he attended High Mass at the cathedral and was deeply moved by the great "clouds of incense and one of Mozart's sublimest masses by an orchestra." At Antwerp, he saw and admired the paintings of Rubens. Everywhere, he ate the most marvelous food: "oysters as

31

small as shrimps, but delicately sweet," "veal chops dressed with a rich sauce piquant," "peas most wonderfully fine" and "salad pre-eminent even among the salads of Flanders which are unique for their delicate crispness and silvery whiteness."

From Brussels it was a short ride to the battlefield of Waterloo where Wellington's victory over Napoleon had taken place only nine years before and where their guide shouted at them in a strange "mixture of Dutch, Flemish, French and English—very rich—forming a kind of Belle Alliance lingo, most likely in compliment to the place."

The three travelers then went to Germany visiting, among other places, Cologne, Mainz, Frankfort and Heidelberg. They were entertained at several of the small courts of Germany, which was at that time a confederation of thirty-eight independent monarchies or states. Benjamin's letters to Sarah recorded all that he did and saw in these places. He told of how military bands played during banquets, of how he and Meredith had been bowling and of how they all greatly enjoyed the excellent Rhenish wine.

Then traveling by boat down the Rhine he experienced a change of purpose. He was staggered by the beauty of the scenery. Its magnificence defied description, and under its spell a sudden liberation came over his spirit. "I determined when descending those magical waters that I would not be a lawyer."

He recorded why he felt that the law was a waste of

time. "The Bar: pooh! law and bad jokes till we are forty; and then with the most brilliant success, the prospect of gout and a coronet." He pictured a typical lawyer as one who is "ever illustrating the obvious, explaining the evident, and expatiating the commonplace."

No. He would not become a lawyer!

# 3 SUDDEN FAME

◆◆◆◆◆◆◆◆◆◆◆◆◆◆◆◆◆◆◆◆◆◆◆◆◆◆◆◆◆◆◆◆◆◆◆◆◆◆◆◆◆◆◆◆◆

RETURNING TO LONDON YOUNG DISRAELI IMMEDI-
ately entered upon an exciting venture. Mexico had just
freed herself from Spain. Bolivia, Peru and Brazil, backed
by England, were also in revolt against their mother
country. British financiers were obtaining mining conces-
sions in these lands, and the English public was rushing
to invest in stock which soared with glittering promise.

Disraeli decided that here was a chance to make a million. He persuaded two friends to join with him. Between
the three of them they scraped together a sum equal to
$35,000 in our modern American currency, and following
a plan devised by Disraeli they began gambling in the
South American stock. For several months all went well.
Their fortunes rose, fluttered and fell only to rise again.

It was a tense and absorbing game. The promise of riches shone brightly, but at the end of seven months and with rude suddenness their dream was shattered. Their stocks crashed and their investment was completely wiped out.

Disraeli's partners were young men of means and the loss of their money did not trouble them. But the twenty-year-old Benjamin had borrowed in order to enter into this speculative venture and what he had borrowed and lost now had to be paid back. But how?

It was to take Disraeli thirty years to wipe out this debt. For thirty years he was to live with its specter. But since all dark clouds have bright sides, Benjamin was to reap some benefits from his folly. He learned a lesson. He never again engaged in wild speculation. He also laughingly said that the kicks he continually received from his debt had the beneficial effect of spurring him on in the race!

With speculation in stocks relegated to the past, Disraeli now entered upon a new field of enterprise. His father's publisher, John Murray, had great admiration for Benjamin, whom he had known since he was a small child. He considered him brilliant and enterprising, and he approached him with a plan.

Murray, who was a book publisher, also published a very successful magazine called *Quarterly Review*. He now wanted to publish a second magazine and asked young Disraeli to become its editor.

Benjamin was delighted with the prospect of entering publishing, but since he was deeply interested in politics, he thought that a daily newspaper would be more important. A newspaper could wield much more political influence than either a weekly or monthly magazine. It could fight for causes, mold public opinion and change the course of events.

He was so enthusiastic about his idea that Murray was soon persuaded to change his plans, and a partnership agreement was signed. Murray was to own half the stock and put up half the capital. Disraeli and a certain Mr. Powles, a friend of Murray's and a financier whom Disraeli had met during his stock adventure, were each to receive a quarter-interest, in return for the remaining half of the needed money.

The terms were simple. There was only one difficulty: Disraeli was not only penniless but heavily in debt. However, a solution was soon found. Powles was to make a down payment on his share of the paper and lend Disraeli enough money to do the same on his share. The rest of the money was to be paid as soon as possible.

With these financial problems out of the way, Murray, Disraeli and Powles now made their plans. Their newspaper would be called the *Representative,* it would compete with *The Times* in dignity and content, and to fulfill Murray's wish, Sir Walter Scott's son-in-law, J. G. Lockhart, would be its editor.

Disraeli now devoted his time exclusively to organizing the company. He attended to a hundred matters such as renting office space, arranging for printing and hiring a staff and correspondents. He proved practical and efficient, yet he was unable to get out the first issue. In December 1825, there was a sharp break on the stock market. A panic ensued. Powles could not raise his and Disraeli's share of the capital, and so Disraeli was forced to give up his cherished post as Murray's right-hand man.

Undaunted by this setback, Murray tried to run the paper alone. However, after six months and the loss of $125,000 he was forced to shut down.

Murray now realized that Disraeli's enthusiasm for politics had led him into a venture which was far too ambitious for a book publisher. However, he did not hold it against his young friend, neither did he condemn him for having failed to raise the promised share of capital.

Disraeli's failure at publishing, following so closely upon his failure at speculation, plunged him into a state of gloom. He was without a job, without money and without prospects. There seemed no direction to his life, and he might have sunk into a state of depression had it not been for the fortunate intervention of a very pretty and accomplished lady called Sarah Austin.

Mrs. Austin and her husband lived close to the D'Israelis, and they had known Benjamin for a number of years. Sarah Austin was a fair musician; she also painted and on occasion tried her hand at literary criticism. Because of this interest in the arts, a bond had grown up between her and Benjamin. Seeing him now in such a miserable state of mind she suggested a magical remedy. Having once read some very fine sketches which he had written about his early youth, she encouraged him to launch upon an autobiographical novel. What was more she promised to show the completed manuscript to one of her friends, a publisher named Colburn.

Disraeli did not feel that he had had enough experience with life to write a novel. He said that his knowledge had been acquired mainly through "books and conversations." But Mrs. Austin persisted and he finally agreed.

His old enthusiasm now returned. He worked without rest, writing at a feverish pace, and at the end of four months he had completed *Vivian Grey*. This, his first novel, was the story of his life at school and of his adventures in speculation and publishing, organized into a work of fiction greatly intensified by his colorful imagination. It was even more, for it gave a vivid and frank description of many celebrities of the day and dramatized Murray's unlucky newspaper venture.

Sarah Austin liked *Vivian Grey* and at once recommended it to Colburn. However, fearing that Colburn might reject it if he knew that it was written by such a young man, she withheld the author's name, a precaution which turned out to be most fortunate. Colburn, entranced by the mystery thus created, decided to capitalize upon it.

He launched upon a prepublication publicity campaign. He said that the book, filled with satirical sketches of well-known people, was the work of an English Don Juan who was personally acquainted with everyone in the London literary sphere. And he whetted the public's appetite by throwing out hints and promises.

*Vivian Grey* was an immediate success. It was the book of the season. Its sarcasm was bold and devastating. Everybody who was anybody bought a copy. Everyone read it and everyone talked about it. All London played a game. "Can you guess?" "Who is this one?" "Who is that one?" and above all, "Who is the author?"

Disraeli found it tremendously exciting being the anonymous author of such a sensational book. He was terribly flattered to overhear strangers on the street, in theatre lobbies and other public places discussing *Vivian Grey*. It was also fun having his friends innocently ask him if he had read the book and who he thought the author might be. Then suddenly all changed. It leaked out that Benjamin Disraeli, a twenty-one-year-old youth was the author, and the literary critics, who had all been silent, now opened up a fierce barrage.

They objected vehemently to the kind of sensationalism displayed in *Vivian Grey*. They also felt that the advance publicity had been undignified. They called the book "shameless," a breach of "good breeding" and said it displayed a "disregard of honorable feeling." Some even went so far as to say that *Vivian Grey* had been written for one purpose only—to make money.

Disraeli had not expected these attacks, and at first dismissed them as coming from second-rate and inferior critics. He waited for the reviews to come in from the best literary journals. He waited especially to hear from the critic of the distinguished Scottish literary magazine, *Blackwood's*. However, when this review arrived it turned out to be more devastating than any other.

Disraeli was stunned. For the first time in his life, he recorded, he became the "subject of the most reckless, the most malignant, and the most adroit ridicule. I was sacrificed, I was scalped." He blamed the critic for not noticing his skillful "satire," his "eloquence," and the expression of his "secret feeling."

He wrote that he was so crushed that the pages "fell from my hand. A film floated over my vision; my knees trembled. I felt that sickness of heart, that we experience in our first serious scrape. I was ridiculous. It was time to die."

However, Disraeli refused to be vanquished. This was no time for self-pity; this was a time for extreme courage. With courage he would win in the end. His belief in courage became so strong at this crucial time that he took "courage" for his motto. He designed a seal for himself which showed a stone tower around which were engraved the words, "Fortitude conquers all difficulties."

Disraeli had tremendous courage. He also had another admirable quality: he never felt bitter or unfriendly to those who rejected or defeated him. Only small men, he said, indulged in pettiness. And so he swallowed his pride. Not once did he show that he had been stunned. Not once did he complain. In fact he displayed that remarkable trait which he described in his grandfather and namesake, Benjamin D'Israeli, "a temper which no disappointment could disturb."

Disraeli presented a brave front, but the shattered hopes, the wide notoriety and the crushing humility which he had experienced as a result of *Vivian Grey* affected his health. He suffered from severe headaches and periods of depression. So he decided to take a trip. A change of scene would do him good. It would give him time to recover his sense of equilibrium.

Fortunately the Austins were going abroad, and they suggested that he join them. They made a happy trio. The Austins found young Disraeli a good traveling companion because he was versed in the history of all the places they visited and was besides always considerate, witty and amusing. Disraeli, on the other hand, enjoyed the intimacy of being with two such devoted friends.

The Austins and Disraeli first visited Paris. Then they journeyed to Switzerland and on to northern Italy: Milan, Verona, Pisa, Padua, Bologna, Turin, Florence, Genoa and finally Venice, the Queen of the Adriatic and home of Marco Polo. Disraeli found Venice fascinating and beautiful. His knowledge of its unique history, its rise from a series of salt marshes into one of the wealthiest and most beautiful cities in the world, its trade with the East and its wars with Constantinople, enriched every moment of his stay. Besides, Venice was the city of his forefathers. There they had found refuge when they were forced to flee from Spain.

He felt that the marble palaces of Venice were the

homes of his ancestors. He later wrote, "I viewed them
with devotion. . . . Within these walls my fathers revelled!
I bowed my head. . . ."

Disraeli and the Austins now crossed over the Alps
and into France and returned to England having visited
eleven of the great cities of Europe.

Disraeli's trip abroad had helped to restore his health.
However, he was in no way cured, and shortly after his
return home he began to suffer from intense headaches
which led to long periods of morbid depression. The doctors diagnosed his state as "inflammation of the brain,"
but they could suggest no remedy. Disraeli decided to go
abroad again on a third trip. This time he wanted to visit
Spain and Greece and then travel through such eastern
lands as Turkey, Egypt and Palestine. Somehow he felt
drawn toward the East, and he had developed a romantic
attachment for Jerusalem and Palestine, the ancient
homeland of his people.

Such a trip would take over a year and would naturally require a good deal of money. Disraeli did not
have any money; he was in fact still deeply in debt. Nor
could his indulgent father provide the necessary funds;
Isaac D'Israeli had recently bought a very expensive
manor house, Brandenham, not far from the town of
Beaconsfield in Buckinghamshire, about twenty-five
miles from London.

Brandenham was beautiful, situated in happy green
country, and there Disraeli joined his family, spending

long hours in the happy company of his sister Sarah and living the life of a country gentleman. He was an excellent horseman, and he spent much time with his horses and dogs. But he did not give up his plans for traveling.

Determined to earn enough money to finance his trip to the East, and encouraged by his devoted sister Sarah, he now projected a sequel to *Vivian Grey.*

Disraeli spent most of his time at Brandenham but he did not give up his friends in London. Neither did he give up his unusual manner of dressing. In fact, his fashions became even more daring. Where he had once worn quiet black velvet suits he now took to colorful clothing, rings, gold chains and jeweled buttons.

He is described as being seen in "green velvet trousers, a canary-colored waistcoat, low shoes, silver buckles, lace at his wrists, and his hair in ringlets."

At another time he was seen walking up Regents Street in a blue topcoat of unusual cut and a pair of light blue trousers.

He himself reported with his usual wit that people seeing him approaching "quite made way for me as I passed. It was like the opening of the Red Sea, which I now perfectly believe from experience."

Disraeli's trips to London were not, however, designed solely to visit friends and startle the public. His interest in politics was one of the main reasons for frequent trips to the city. He wanted to listen to the speakers in the Houses of Parliament: such men as Macaulay, Shiel, Canning and Peel. He recorded his impressions. "Mr.

Peel . . . is fluent without the least style. Canning . . . a consummate rhetorician . . . a dash of commonplace in all that he said." Then in a letter to his sister he wrote, "Macaulay admirable; but, between ourselves, I could floor them all. . . . I could carry everything before me in that House. The time will come. . . ."

He then continued with his evaluation, "One thing is quite clear—that a man may speak very well in the House of Commons, and fail very completely in the House of Lords. There are two distinct styles requisite; I intend, in the course of my career, if I have time, to give a specimen of both. In the Lower House, *Don Juan* may perhaps be our model; in the Upper House, *Paradise Lost.*"

Disraeli's new novel was called *Young Duke.* It proved to be a clever picture of high society but it did not have the boldness and brilliant dazzle of his first book. His friend the novelist Bulwer Lytton, who was only a year older than Disraeli, read the manuscript and suggested places where it might be improved. But Disraeli was impatient. He wanted money at once and so he decided to submit it just as it was. He sold it to Colburn for 500 pounds.

Disraeli now had some money toward his trip, but not enough. He naturally had to give some of his 500 pounds to his creditors. However, his friends the Austins came to his rescue; they lent him 500 pounds. This made everything possible. And his good friend William Meredith, who had independent means and who was engaged to his beloved sister Sarah, joined him.

They left London by steamer on May 28, 1830. They knew that they were going to lands where traveling was difficult and beset with dangers. Bandits made a good living on lonely highways. And so they took little luggage with them. However, among their cases there was a "little red bag" which Disraeli's mother had sewn for him. In this bag Disraeli carried two pistols.

Disraeli and Meredith went first to Gibraltar. Making this British fortress their headquarters they then traveled through southern Spain visiting Cadiz, Seville, Cordova and Granada.

They traveled on horseback sometimes for ten hours a day. The constant danger of bandits and cutthroats created a high degree of adventure, every minute of which Disraeli enjoyed.

He equally enjoyed the effect his outlandish clothing made upon the people. "I have also the fame of being the first who has passed the Straits with two canes, a morning and an evening cane. I change my canes as the gun fires." And since the men and women of Spain carried fans, he had one too. "I also have my fan, which makes my cane extremely jealous."

In another letter he says that his black curls attracted the attention of the Spanish women who thought he was wearing a wig. "I was obliged to let them pull it to satisfy their curiosity."

However, the pleasure he derived from all this was

somewhat diminished by the sudden news of the death of King George IV. In respect for his dead monarch Disraeli left off wearing fancy waistcoats. A sacrifice which he says showed how "I truly grieve."

Disraeli enjoyed immensely the attention he was attracting, but he also enjoyed the people, country and cities of Spain. Everywhere he went he was reminded of Don Quixote. His enthusiasm was so great when he visited the Alhambra, repeating over and over, "This is my palace," that the old lady who served as guide thought he was a Moor.

He was in high spirits, and with all the excitement and sunshine his health improved. Just before leaving Spain he wrote, "The air of the mountains, the rising sun, the rising appetite, the variety of picturesque persons and things we met, and the impending danger made a delightful life. . . . Never have I been better."

However, he missed his family, and he begged Sarah for more news of home. "Write me about Brandenham, about dogs and horses, orchards, gardens, who calls, where you go, who my father sees in London, what is said."

From Spain Disraeli and Meredith headed eastward. After a very rough sea voyage they finally reached the Island of Malta. There Disraeli donned Spanish dress, embroidered jacket, white trousers and a multicolored sash, and went to pay his respects to the English governor! Beholding him, this staid gentleman burst into a roar of laughter, which immediately sealed a bond of friendship between them.

Here at Malta, the two young travelers ran into an acquaintance, James Clay, who hired a yacht and took them aboard as paying guests. Together, with Tita, a manservant who had once been Lord Byron's gondolier, the three Englishmen set sail for Corfu, one of the islands off the coast of Greece. This time, just for the fun of it, Disraeli dressed as a Greek pirate.

They went on to Turkey which Disraeli found like a scene from *The Arabian Nights*. He liked the crowded narrow streets and open markets, the veiled women, the camel caravans and the flashing smiles of the Arabs. He also liked the slow pace of life. He seemed to fit in perfectly with the life in this foreign land. His own heritage was Oriental. And this sympathy of spirit which he felt with the Turks was to play an important role in the destiny of Europe.

Setting sail once more and dodging some real pirates Disraeli, Meredith and James Clay now visited the Ionian Islands, Athens and other historic landmarks in Greece. From there they went to Constantinople, the great city where West meets East. Then on to Palestine. They landed at Jaffa and "well mounted and well armed" they traveled inland to Jerusalem.

"I was thunderstruck," wrote Disraeli describing his first glimpse of the Holy City. "Except Athens I never saw anything more essentially striking. . . ."

Disraeli knew the history of his ancient people, and he was deeply moved by everything about him. He visited the tombs of the kings of Israel, trod the ground David had trod, stood lost in dream before the scant remains of the city's ancient walls and visited the Holy Sepulchre. He who was now a Christian liked to think of Christ as a Hebrew prince; he could not accept the division between the two great faiths which worshipped the same God.

Disraeli, Meredith and Clay reached Egypt in March 1831. They stayed in Alexandria for four months, during which time they took many trips to see the wonders of Egypt's past. They climbed the Great Pyramid and sailed up the Nile to visit the ruins about the ancient capital of Thebes.

"Conceive a feverish and tumultuous dream," Disraeli wrote home, "full of triumphal gates, processions of paintings, interminable walls of heroic sculpture, granite colossi of gods and kings, prodigious obelisks, avenues of sphinxes, and halls of a thousand columns thirty feet in girth and of proportionate height." Thus he summed up the full glory of ancient Egypt.

But Disraeli was destined also to know a very different Egypt—modern Egypt. Walking one day through the gardens surrounding the royal palace in Cairo, he suddenly came upon Pasha Mehemet, himself, ruler of Egypt. The little pasha, who had a fine white beard and sharp eyes, was playing chess with his court jester, and being a great admirer of all things European he stopped Disraeli and had him visit with him. This first meeting led to several audiences in which Disraeli learned that the pasha was not only ruler of Egypt but also its sole landlord and merchant. He owned everything and was trying desperately to modernize his country by building factories and by creating a great army after the manner of European countries. However, his ambition was surpassed only by his ignorance and tyranny. And so everything the pasha tried failed, and the people of Egypt were being ground deeper and deeper into the sands of their ancient land.

So it was that before Disraeli left the ancient land of the Pharaohs he knew Egypt. This knowledge was in later years to prove of great value to England.

The grand tour was now over. Disraeli had seen everything that he wanted to see and he longed for England and home. He humorously summed up his adventurous journey with the words, "Like all great travelers, I have seen more than I remember and remember more than I have seen."

He had remarked sometime back in a letter to his family, "A mingled picture of domestic enjoyment and fresh butter, from both of which I have been so long estranged, daily flits across my fancy." This image now grew more vivid. But just when all arrangements for the homeward journey had been completed, Meredith became sick. He contracted smallpox, and died after only a few days of illness.

Disraeli was plunged into the deepest agony. His grief

at losing his closest and dearest friend was increased a hundredfold by the thought of the sorrow which his letter, bearing the tragic news, would bring to his sister, Sarah. She and Meredith were to have been married immediately after his return to England, and plans for the wedding had all been completed.

# 4 THE LION OF DUKE STREET

◆◆◆◆◆◆◆◆◆◆◆◆◆◆◆◆◆◆◆◆◆◆◆◆◆◆◆◆◆◆◆◆◆◆◆◆◆◆◆◆◆◆◆◆◆

RETURNING FROM HIS EASTERN TRIP IN OCTOBER OF 1831, Disraeli found England in a state of unrest. Factory workers were chafing under long hours and low wages. There were riots in many factory cities. And the people were demanding that outdated voting laws be changed and the franchise extended.

Representation in Parliament had been granted to the shires or counties, boroughs and cities during the reign of Elizabeth I, almost three hundred years before. The system by which these representatives were elected had not been materially changed since that time, and so shocking inequalities existed. No adjustments had been made for the shift of population and the rise of new social classes during the Industrial Revolution. "Pocket boroughs," controlled by the crown or large landowners, and "rotten boroughs," where the population had greatly declined, sent two representatives to Parliament, while big industrial cities like Manchester and Birmingham had no representatives at all. Out of a population of 24,000,000 in 1831 only about 400,000 were qualified to vote. Besides, there was widespread corruption; the sale of votes and seats was commonplace.

A reform bill had been presented to the House of Lords while Disraeli was abroad, but it had been argued away on the ground that it was not liberal enough, upholding too strongly the traditions of aristocratic England. On the eve of Disraeli's return another more liberal reform bill had been introduced, and the public was awaiting tensely the results of the debates.

Such was the temper of the time. And it was this temper that decided Disraeli. He had always wanted to enter politics, and this seemed the proper moment. However, there were several difficulties confronting him. He did not belong to an old landed English family. He did not have enough money to buy votes. And he was neither a Whig, who believed in popular rights, nor a Tory, a conservative. He disliked what both of these parties stood for and so he decided to run as an independent from High Wycombe, a "pocket borough" close to Brandenham. It registered some thirty-two votes and elected one representative. A candidate did not have to run from the district in which he lived; he could run from any district which would accept him.

Disraeli campaigned ardently, saying that he stood for only one thing: England. He further proclaimed he was a man of the people; and he promised that if elected he would ease the lot of the poor—a strange idea to advance, since the poor of High Wycombe were landless and therefore did not have the vote.

Between his "independence" and his humanitarian promises Disraeli lost the election. This marked his first political defeat, and although he was deeply disappointed, he took it calmly, as he was to take all his subsequent defeats. He decided that he would try again at the next election.

Having time on his hands Disraeli took up his pen once more. His experience in the East had given him a lot of material which he wanted to record. And so he launched into another autobiographical novel entitled *Contarini Fleming*.

The hero of this volume ran away from school because, having a poet's soul, he could not bear the strict controls imposed upon him. He later entered politics and wrote a satirical book which caused a tremendous sensation. After that he traveled. Following Byron's example he went first to Venice and then to many of the places from which Disraeli himself had just returned: Greece, Turkey, Spain, Palestine and Egypt.

This work, on the whole, was one of great beauty, and this time the critics were truly impressed. One distinguished reviewer thought it equal to Byron's *Childe*

*Harold* and the great German author Goethe sent Disraeli glowing compliments. It was also acclaimed by Heinrich Heine.

*Contarini Fleming* was a literary success, but a financial failure. Disraeli was not disheartened by this and immediately began writing another novel, this time in poetic prose. It was called *Alroy* and, while autobiographical, was inspired by a Jewish hero of the twelfth century called David Alroy, whose story had always fascinated Disraeli.

This novel with its Eastern setting was also very well received. The critics thought it original, full of interesting ideas and written in an easy and delightful style. Disraeli's place in the London literary world was now established.

With *Vivian Grey* Disraeli had received sensational notoriety, but now he had genuine literary recognition and he became the lion of London. Everybody wanted to meet him. He took an apartment on Duke Street and was a guest in every house of distinction in fashionable Mayfair.

He met such men as Lord Durham, a leading Whig; Lord Lyndhurst, a leading Tory; and a very young under secretary of state named William Gladstone. Sir Robert Peel, a leader in Parliament, was also one of his acquaintances, as was the most popular man in all England, the Duke of Wellington, the hero of Waterloo.

While these men were rather repelled by Disraeli's cutting wit and artificial manners, especially in the matter of dress, they could not help liking him for his brilliant mind and profound knowledge of history and government. The ladies, however, liked him without reservations.

He became the favorite of the three most beautiful women in London, sisters and the granddaughters of Sheridan the playwright: Mrs. Norton, Mrs. Blackwood and Lady Seymour. The aged Lady Cork, who knew everyone of note, also adored him. And one of his most intimate friends was Lady Blessington, a wealthy widow and bad novelist who had known Lord Byron.

In fact, there was not a lady in Mayfair who did not strive to meet him. A certain Mrs. Wyndham Lewis, wife of a member of Parliament, was very eager. Seeing him one evening at a party at the home of his friend Bulwer Lytton, she asked her host to introduce him. It was an act of destiny. This casual introduction was to prove the most important event in his life, but Disraeli gave little thought to it at the time.

Writing next day to Sarah, Disraeli described Mrs. Wyndham Lewis as "a pretty little woman, a flirt and a rattle." He said that she hardly stopped talking for a moment. "She told me she liked silent, melancholy men. I answered that 'I had no doubt of it.'"

Toward the end of 1832 the Reform Bill was finally passed. It redistributed some of the seats in Parliament according to population, simplified voting procedures and extended the franchise in the boroughs and counties to all those landless people who paid ten pounds or more a year rent for their homes or places of business. This gave the vote to many tenant farmers, shopkeepers and craftsmen.

A new election was immediately called, and Disraeli decided to run again in High Wycombe. This time he announced loudly that while he was still an independent he was also a conservative and a radical. "A conservative to preserve what is good in the constitution, and a radical to remove what is bad." But these words did not work magic and he was once more defeated, getting 119 to his opponents 140 votes.

Defeated but not vanquished Disraeli was now more determined than ever to distingish himself in politics. He was, in fact, so fired by this wish that he could think of little else. When Lord Melbourne, then home secretary, met him at a party and asked him, "Well now, tell me, what do you want to be?" he replied very seriously, "I want to be prime minister."

Lord Melbourne was naturally startled. Recovering he tried to explain to the young man that such a thing was completely impossible. "You must put all these foolish notions out of your head. . . ."

However, four years later and just before he died, Lord Melbourne seems to have changed his mind. Hearing that Disraeli had just become leader in the House of Commons, he exclaimed, "By God! the fellow will do it yet."

While waiting for the next opportunity to run for office Disraeli divided his time between Brandenham and London. At Brandenham he returned to his horses, dogs, books and writing, but in London he was swept along in the social current. "I make my way easily in the highest set where there is no envy, malice . . . and where they like . . . to be amused."

An American who met him at Lady Blessington's records that Disraeli was wearing "patent leather pumps, a white stick with a black cord and tassel, and a quantity of chains about his neck and pockets . . ." But this gentleman saw more. He said, "He has one of the most remarkable faces I ever saw. He is lividly pale. . . . His mouth is alive . . . and when he has burst forth, as he does constantly . . . I might as well attempt to gather up the foam of the sea as to convey an idea of the extraordinary language in which he clothed his descriptions. He talked like a racehorse approaching the winning post, every muscle in action. . . . His command of language was truly wonderful, his powers of sarcasm unsurpassed."

Mrs. Wyndham Lewis was one of those who shared this American gentleman's opinion of Benjamin Disraeli. She shared it without reservation. In spite of the fact that she was twelve years older than Disraeli and that he had once deplored her idle chatter, in spite of the fact that she did not belong to the highest society and dressed in a rather freakish manner and that she was uneducated and did not know which came first, the Greeks or the Romans, Disraeli now found himself greatly attracted to her.

He often visited Mr. and Mrs. Wyndham Lewis in

their home in fashionable Park Lane in London. They in turn occasionally went to Brandenham with Disraeli to visit his family.

In fact, their friendship soon grew so close and warm that Mrs. Wyndham Lewis used a nickname for Disraeli, one that would remain with him for the rest of his life, one that, in a short time, would be used affectionately by millions. She called him Dizzy.

Disraeli ran for a third time from High Wycombe during the general election of 1835, and this time while he was still an independent, he had the endorsement of the most distinguished Tory in England, the Duke of Wellington. It was just twenty years since the Iron Duke's victory at Waterloo for which the grateful nation had given him a gift of 400,000 pounds and a fine country estate. During these twenty years the Duke had entered politics and had served for a short time as prime minister. No candidate running for office could have had a better sponsor. Yet Disraeli did not win.

He worked hard, made many speeches and spent long hours going from door to door talking personally with the voters, but it did not help. His appearance worked against him: his fancy vests, his gold chains and rings, his pale face framed by jet black hair, his dark penetrating eyes—all this created a picture so different from that of the usual English candidate, that even though his speeches were convincing and moving the voters regarded him with suspicion.

Disraeli was disappointed but not discouraged. He would win next time. To console himself he now wrote a pamphlet explaining his political philosophy. It was entitled "Vindication of the English Constitution in a Letter to a Noble and Learned Lord, by Disraeli the Younger," and in it he presented the view that the House of Lords should remain as it was but that the House of Commons should be revamped. He said that although the lords held their seats through birth and not through popular election, still the House of Lords had been tried through the centuries and had proven to serve all England. The House of Commons, on the other hand, did not represent the masses because not enough people had the vote. He suggested that a new "reform bill" be enacted to give the vote to many more people. In short he said that it was the duty of all forward-looking political leaders to defend the past insofar as it was a living past and to cleanse their parties of prejudices and outworn principles. Above all it was their duty to support the common people.

The pamphlet was a tremendous success. Disraeli received wide acclaim. Both the Duke of Wellington and Sir Robert Peel sent him congratulations. But his most ardent admirer was his own father, old Isaac D'Israeli. He wrote his son: "You have now a positive name and being in the great political world, which you had not ten days ago. You never wanted for genius but it was apt to run over. You have rejected the curt and flashy diction which betrayed continual effort. All now flows in one continuous stream of thought and expression—at once masculine and graceful."

Disraeli now realized that in order to get elected he must join one party or the other, the Whigs or the Tories. Since his sponsor the Duke of Wellington was a Tory and since Sir Robert Peel who was now prime minister was also a Tory and advocated many progressive measures of which he approved, Disraeli decided to join with the Tories.

He applied for membership in the Tories' exclusive Carlton Club, and was accepted with open arms. The Tories recognized that Disraeli's voice and pen would be assets to the party. He was soon dining with the party leaders "on swan, very white and tender, and stuffed with truffles" and enlivening their conversation.

The party did not wait long. At the first opportunity they put up Disraeli to champion the Tory cause in Taunton, against a Whig candidate who was an established politician. It was hardly a fair contest and for the fourth time, Disraeli was defeated.

However, he had won in other ways. It had been a hot fight and had been reported almost daily in the papers, and so his reputation had been broadened. His political opinions were now known to a wide audience. He was often quoted. One thing above all that had brought him renown and the admiration of the public was his personal defense against a despicable attack by Daniel O'Connell, one of the leaders for Irish independence.

O'Connell had publicly said of Disraeli, "He is a liar.

. . . He is the most degraded of his species . . . a reptile.
His name shows he is of Jewish origin. . . . He displays
some of the lowest and most disgusting grade of moral
turpitude. . . . He possesses just the qualities of the im-
penitent thief on the Cross, whose name, I verily believe,
must have been Disraeli."

Disraeli challenged O'Connell to a duel. O'Connell,
who had just killed one man in a duel, refused. Since he
could not thus defend his honor, Disraeli denounced
O'Connell in speeches and in the press through a series of
letters.

Old Isaac D'Israeli and Sarah were distressed by the
whole affair. However, the Duke of Wellington expressed
the opinion of the majority when he said, "It is the most
manly thing. . . . When will he come into Parliament?"

While awaiting another chance to run for office, Disraeli returned to the gay social life of London. He spent
his time at parties, balls and receptions. Then suddenly
one night in June 1837 everything changed. King William IV died and an eighteen-year-old girl called Victoria became queen of England.

This meant a new election. It meant that Disraeli could
run again. Although he did not know it, it also meant that
the moment he had hoped for so ardently had arrived, for
destiny had decreed that Victoria and Disraeli should
begin their careers at the same time.

However, there was another lady who also played an
important part in Disraeli's life at this moment. She was

the one who called him Dizzy. Disraeli was now so popular that seven districts invited him to run as their candidate, but it was the pretty little Mrs. Wyndham Lewis who won out. While she was rather uneducated and uncultured she nevertheless had one definite talent—she possessed a keen political sense. She induced Dizzy to be one of the candidates from her husband's district, the city of Maidstone, not far from London.

Maidstone was entitled to two seats in the Commons. Her husband was a Tory. Dizzy was a Tory. And there was only one candidate, a Whig, running in opposition. Victory seemed almost certain.

It was. To fill its two seats the people of Maidstone elected Wyndham Lewis and Benjamin Disraeli.

Mrs. Wyndham Lewis was very happy. She wrote to her brother, "Mark what I say—mark what I prophesie: Mr. Disraeli will in a very few years be one of the greatest men of his day."

# 5 DIZZY'S MAIDEN SPEECH AND MARRIAGE

❖❖❖❖❖❖❖❖❖❖❖❖❖❖❖❖❖❖❖❖❖❖❖❖❖❖❖❖❖❖❖❖❖❖❖❖❖

ALTHOUGH DISRAELI WAS ELECTED TO OFFICE DURING the summer of 1837, Queen Victoria's first Parliament did not convene until the middle of November. He was, therefore, forced to wait several months before taking his coveted seat. Finally the day he had dreamed of since early childhood arrived, and together with the other members of the House of Commons he went to the House of Lords, as is the custom, to hear the queen deliver her opening speech to Parliament.

Returning to the House of Commons after this moving ceremony, Disraeli took a seat close to Sir Robert Peel, who was now the leader of the Tory opposition. Peel welcomed Dizzy. He was happy to have him on his side, for he knew that his power of speech, his wit and sarcasm would be very deadly to his political enemies. Besides, Dizzy had the courage to speak out.

During his campaigns Disraeli had been very outspoken on many subjects, especially those related to social reforms. He had challenged the Poor Law which the Whigs had recently enacted, on the grounds that this law gave relief to the destitute by establishing workhouses. Workhouses he felt were degrading and evil. "This act has disgraced the country," he cried. "It announces to the world that in England poverty is a crime."

Disraeli had also expressed criticism of Lord Melbourne, the prime minister, who was very old-fashioned in his political ideas. He was a kind of political roadblock to progress. This attitude was objectionable to Dizzy, especially since Lord Melbourne was extremely close to the young queen, advising her on all subjects. During the first months of her reign, the queen leaned completely on his judgment, following all his instructions.

With such attacks already on record, Peel naturally expected great things from Disraeli, and he was not to be disappointed. However, for the first few days, Disraeli just sat and listened. He wanted to become acquainted with procedure and learn how the other members felt and deported themselves. And so he listened patiently to long debates delivered by members of the different hostile camps which divided the House of Commons: Whig, Tory, independent and radical.

Disraeli was extremely interested in all the questions of the day, and since he was not personally involved in any of the problems discussed, he enjoyed freedom of opinion. He owned no land. He was not connected with trade. Nor was he an industrialist who owned factories and employed labor. And he cared little for the medieval English traditions that many of his colleagues were eager to preserve.

This lack of personal ties was of great political advantage to Disraeli. Since he had no loyalties to support, he was free to judge all bills on their merits.

Disraeli was politically free, and yet a heavy load hung over him—his personal debts.

The political campaigns he had waged had been costly. Having no party to back him when he ran three times as an independent in High Wycombe, he had been forced to pay all expenses out of his own pocket. His extravagant social life had also cost more money than he could earn.

From where did Disraeli's money come? His books and articles brought in practically nothing. Not wishing to involve his friends he was forced to go to professional moneylenders.

Since Disraeli did not own land or securities to offer as collateral, these professional moneylenders gambled on his future. They had faith in Dizzy's talents—by this time, almost everyone in London, even the artists who drew caricatures for the papers, was calling him Dizzy. They believed he would be successful, and their loans would be repaid. However, their risk was great and so they charged a high rate of interest, 8 per cent. When his notes came due and he wanted them renewed, he had to pay 10 per cent interest and even more. Then the interest had to be paid in full before he could borrow more money.

In time his finances became so complicated that he did not know the exact amount of his debts. It is estimated that when he took his seat in Parliament he owed a sum equal to $100,000.

A few weeks after Parliament was opened by young Queen Victoria, Dizzy rose to make his maiden speech. The subject was the thorny question of Irish independence, and he was given the floor following Daniel O'Connell, the Irish leader who had attacked him because of his Jewish ancestry and whom Disraeli had vanquished with his pen.

A first speech in the House of Commons is usually heard in respectful silence. But it was not so on this day. O'Connell's followers and the Whigs whom O'Connell supported joined to make trouble for Dizzy. It mattered not what he said, they interrupted with heckling, catcalls, barnyard noises and boisterous laughter. But he was not put off; he remained unruffled. He waited for silence, and when the silence came he started again. But so did the hoots and calls. Finally realizing that it was impossible to have quiet, he talked on unheard just to use up the time allotted to him.

At length ending his speech, he added in a clear voice that could be heard by all, "I am not at all surprised at the reception I have experienced. I have begun things many times, and have succeeded though many had predicted that I must fail. . . ."

There was more laughter and calls. The din became overwhelming. Then suddenly silence descended, freezing all in their places, because above all the racket they heard these words spoken in a voice described as almost terrifying, "I will sit down now, but the time will come when you *will* hear me."

Having a temperament which "no disappointment could disturb," Disraeli was not disheartened by this ugly experience. Yet he listened to advice from a battle-hardened politician whom he happened to meet at a dinner party given by his friend Bulwer Lytton.

This man advised him to forget that he was a "genius" and, in order to show that he had not been cowed, to speak soon again. This man further advised Disraeli to "Speak often. Be very quiet; try to be dull . . . quote figures, dates. In a short time the House will sigh for the wit and eloquence they know are in you."

This was good advice and Disraeli followed it.

His second speech was mildly cheered. In a letter to Sarah he predicted, "Next time I rise in the House, I shall sit down amidst loud cheers." And he was right.

Disraeli's third speech was in support of a new copyright law. Being an author, this was a subject about which he knew a great deal. He had good reasons for proposing that the copyright on an author's work should be extended for the full lifetime of the author plus sixty years to protect his heirs. At that time the copyright in

England lasted only twenty-eight years or for the lifetime of the author, whichever was longer.

Disraeli spoke with logic and feeling. The entire House applauded and cheered, including his party leader Sir Robert Peel.

In March 1838, only a few months after Disraeli had taken his seat in Parliament, a very sad thing occurred. His friend Mr. Wyndham Lewis, who had helped him gain his seat, fell ill and died.

Mrs. Wyndham Lewis was grief-stricken. Dizzy tried to console her. He offered his advice, assistance and companionship if needed and begged her not to indulge unduly in sorrow. "You are too young to feel that life has not yet a fresh spring of felicity in store," he wrote.

The coronation of Queen Victoria was to take place in June. Mrs. Wyndham Lewis had fully intended to witness this colorful ceremony in the Abbey, but being in deep mourning for her husband she was unable to do so.

As a member of Parliament Dizzy had received an invitation, but he also decided that he would not attend, although he loved colorful pageants. The reason? He did not have the proper clothes!

He had plenty of clothes for other occasions but not for a coronation. He needed knee breeches, silk stockings and the rest of the prescribed court dress. These things could easily be bought, but he had no money and hesitated to borrow still more.

To console himself he made light of the whole affair.

"What for?" he asked. "To get up early at eight o'clock, to sit dressed like a flunkey in the Abbey for seven or eight hours and to listen to a sermon by the Bishop of London, can be no great enjoyment."

This is what he said. But inwardly he felt that he would be missing something. Coronations occur only rarely. And so at the very last moment, at two-thirty in the morning, he bought the necessary court attire and attended the function.

He enjoyed the coronation to the fullest. While poking fun at his political foe Lord Melbourne, the prime minister, for officiating "with his coronet cocked over his nose, his robes under his feet and holding the great sword of State like a butcher," he nevertheless found the pageant "without exception the most splendid, various and interesting affair at which I ever was present."

The solemn music, the ancient rites, the gowns of the nobility made of velvets and satins trimmed with ermine, silver and gold, the jewels, the coronets, the joyous ringing of the bells, all stirred Disraeli's sense of the dramatic. And when it was over he called upon Mrs. Wyndham Lewis to describe everything which had taken place and to present her with the gold commemorative medal which he had received as a member of Parliament. Mr. Wyndham Lewis would have received one had he lived. And since both the Lewis' had done so much to further his career, Disraeli wanted Mrs. Lewis to accept his medal as though it were her husband's.

Two weeks later Disraeli witnessed another event, a

71

colorful military review. It was held in Hyde Park and he viewed it from the windows of Mrs. Wyndham Lewis' house across the way in Park Lane.

He was now a frequent visitor at Mrs. Lewis'. In fact, he called upon her almost every day, and their friends began to whisper about romance. But Mrs. Lewis had other suitors, and besides certain barriers existed between her and Dizzy. In the first place, Mrs. Lewis was forty-five years old and Dizzy only thirty-three. Then, she was very rich while he had nothing but debts; her husband had left her the fine house in Park Lane and a yearly income equal to $20,000 a princely sum in those days. There was also a difference in temperament. As she herself confessed, she was superficial, a chatterbox, undependable and easily bored. Dizzy was just the opposite.

Though both were on guard against emotional involvements, their friendship grew deeper with each day. On the days he did not see her, he wrote her long letters, just like those he wrote to Sarah, letters filled with details about his life. Some spoke of his successes in the House: "Every paper in London, Radical, Whig or Tory, has spoken of my speech in the highest terms. . . ." Other letters gave detailed descriptions of parties and receptions which he had attended. Nothing was omitted: the ladies' gowns and jewels, the potted orange trees, the glassware, the caviar, pheasants, rare wines and cheeses.

Disraeli had known many brilliant women, but in Mary Anne, as he now called her, he found the companion for whom he longed. Others found her stupid and frivolous, but not he. He knew that she had another side. She was good-humored and honest. She understood men and politics. Her judgment on both was sound. She was steadfast; whatever she undertook she did well and thoroughly. And she was feminine, warm and devoted. Besides, he knew that she admired him greatly. And so he wanted her to be his wife.

Mary Anne, however, hesitated. In respect for her late husband she wanted to wait a full year before remarrying. Besides, some of her friends, especially Mrs. Bulwer Lytton, suspected that Dizzy wanted to marry her for her money, and were quick to say so. She suggested that a separation might test their true feelings for each other. Therefore, with Parliament in recess, Disraeli went to Brandenham, where he set to work writing a tragedy.

Each day Disraeli sent Mary Anne a long letter telling of his work and expressing his love. "I think my present work will far exceed expectations." In another letter he wrote, "I look upon my creation and see that it is good." In still another letter he said, "I envy the gentlemen about you, but I am not jealous. When the eagle leaves you the vultures return. . . . There is hardly a flower to be found, but I have sent you a few sweet peas."

After a short time his separation from her began to torment him. He wrote:

> I cannot reconcile love and separation. My ideas of love are the perpetual enjoyment of the society of the sweet being to whom I am devoted, the sharing of every thought

73

and even every fancy, of every charm and every care. . . .
I wish to be with you, to live with you, never to be away
from you—I care not where, in heaven or on earth, or in
the waters under the earth.

This was a touching plea; however, Mary Anne was not
moved. She insisted that their separation continue. Disraeli reluctantly agreed. But when her letters became
fewer and fewer and their warm tone changed, he could
bear it no longer. He hurried to London to see her.

Exactly what took place between them that day no one
knows. However, from the letter Disraeli wrote to Mary
Anne immediately after leaving her, it can be assumed
that she feared he might be marrying her for her money
and to elevate himself socially. Her friends had apparently filled her mind with ugly suspicions.

Disraeli's letter shows very clearly how hurt he was:

By heavens, as far as worldly interests are concerned,
your alliance could not benefit me. All that society can
offer is at my command. . . . I can live, as I live, without
disgrace, until the inevitable progress of events gives me
that independence which is all I require. I have entered
into these ungracious details because you reproached me
with my interested views. No; I would not condescend to
be the minion of a princess; and not all the gold of Ophir
should ever lead me to the altar.

He then went on to say that she had broken his spirit,
outraged his heart and tainted his honor. He concluded
with these words:

74

Farewell. I will not affect to wish you happiness, for it is not in your nature to obtain it. For a few years you may flutter in some frivolous circle. But the time will come when you will sigh for any heart that could be fond, and despair of one that can be faithful. . . . Then you will recall to your memory the passionate heart that you have forfeited. . . .

Receiving this letter, Mary Anne suddenly realized how foolish she had been and how much Dizzy really meant to her. The prospect of the future without him was unbearable. Completely distracted she wrote: "For God's sake come to me. . . . I will answer all you wish. I never desired you to leave the house, or implied or thought a word about money. . . . I am devoted to you."

Dizzy and Mary Anne's quarrel and reconciliation had strengthened their devotion to each other and determined their future. Disraeli returned to Parliament in the best possible state of mind.

He had once predicted that a time would come when the House would be eager to hear him speak. That time had now arrived. On a number of occasions when several members rose simultaneously to take the floor, shouts came from different parts of the house, "Dizzy! Dizzy! Let us hear from Dizzy!"

No longer were there noisy catcalls, derisive laughter and ugly heckling. When he rose to speak, all was now quiet so that not a single word would be missed.

Disraeli always spoke boldly and expressed his honest

75

opinions. He often opposed acts because he could see in them what others failed to see—harmful future results. It was because of his foresight, for instance, that during this particular session of Parliament he opposed a bill for state education, even though he firmly believed in education for the masses.

Disraeli opposed this particular education bill because he said that "it could be used for evil purposes by an evil government." He foresaw clearly that the kind of education provided for in this particular bill was the kind of education which could warp the minds of all the young people of the nation, changing the character of the land for evil. In this he was a whole century before his time. It was both a warning and a prophecy.

What Disraeli had to say was now listened to with interest and respect. Referring to a speech which he delivered at this time, Dizzy was able to write to his sister, Sarah, "The complete command of the House I now have is remarkable . . . nothing can describe to you the mute silence which immediately ensued as I rose, broken only by members hurrying to their places to listen."

Mary Anne had insisted upon waiting a whole year before remarrying. But when this time had passed, Disraeli still did not propose formally.

Recalling this whole period in her life in later years, Mary Anne confided in an intimate friend, "I had many admirers who wanted to marry me, but I knew they were all thinking of my money and not of myself. There was one exception to this, namely Dizzy. I knew that he was in love with me and not with my money because he showed his affection and love to me while my first husband was alive . . . He was evidently attached to me, and wished to propose, but was embarrassed by the difference in our fortunes. One day he spent some time with me but did not come to the point. I brought the matter to a head by laying my hand on his and saying, 'Why should not we two put our two fortunes together?' and thus it came about that we were engaged."

They were married on August 28, 1839, in St. George's Church, Hanover Square. Mary Anne recorded this fact in her neatly kept account book. She wrote, "Dear Dizzy became my husband."

A few days later they left England for a three-month tour of Europe. They went first to Baden-Baden, then through the Black Forest to Stuttgart and on to Munich, Nuremburg and Frankfort. Their trip ended in Paris, where Mary Anne evidently bought herself some dresses, for Dizzy wrote home to say that she looked "like Madame de Pompadour."

Returning to London in November they went directly to Mary Anne's beautiful house in Park Lane. This was to be Dizzy's home for the next thirty-three years.

# 6 OF PRINCES AND PAUPERS

❖❖❖❖❖❖❖❖❖❖❖❖❖❖❖❖❖❖❖❖❖❖❖❖❖❖❖❖❖❖❖❖❖❖❖

DIZZY'S MARRIAGE TO MARY ANNE WAS MOST SUC-
cessful. They adored each other. She was convinced that
Dizzy was the greatest man in all England, and her faith
gave him an inner strength. He, on the other hand, found
her to be the "perfect wife."

Mary Anne might have endless faults in the eyes of
others, but she was the very person Disraeli needed. She
recognized that his serious expression, caustic wit and
outlandish manner of dress were only defenses. She
knew that behind this façade was a sensitive, gentle and
brilliant person. And she provided a refuge for him from
that hostile world he had known ever since he entered
the school at Blackheath when a little boy.

Disraeli and Mary Anne were inseparable. She went

everywhere with him, and her open adoration of him and naïve remarks caused much amusement to their friends and acquaintances. She waited on him slavishly, constantly trying to arrange things for his comfort and pleasure. And she made the most surprising remarks. At a party one evening she said, "Dizzy has the most wonderful moral courage, but no physical courage. When he has his shower-bath, I always have to pull the string." Because of such behavior and remarks people looked upon her as being rather ridiculous. Dizzy knew this but he did not care; he loved Mary Anne so dearly that nothing could alter his feelings.

His family also adored her. She and he often went to Brandenham, and her cheerfulness and laughter brightened the great house which was now invaded by sorrow, for old Isaac D'Israeli was going blind.

But Dizzy's marriage to Mary Anne was not the only happy union in England. Just five months after the Disraelis were married, London celebrated the wedding of Queen Victoria to the German prince, Albert of Saxe-Coburg. This marriage was also destined to be very successful. Victoria and Albert loved each other dearly, and in time had nine beautiful children.

England was in a state of social and economic crisis. The land was wealthy and yet abject poverty was to be seen on every side. The extremes between those who, like Prince Albert, had $150,000 a year for pocket money, awarded him by Parliament, and those who were starving were too great.

How had this condition come about?

The invention of the condensing steam engine by James Watt in 1769 had revolutionized all of the Western world, England in particular. During the seventy years which had elapsed since that momentous day, England had changed from a purely agricultural country into a country with large industrial centers.

With steam engines for power, ocean-going vessels quickly traveled the sea lanes between England and her far-flung colonies in all parts of the world. They brought the raw materials home to be manufactured and carried them back to ready markets in the colonies and in independent foreign lands. Profits poured in at an ever-increasing rate. Factories, also powered by steam engines, grew ever larger and multiplied with the speed of magic.

England had plenty of coal to feed the engines and iron to build more machines. Great manufacturing centers like Leeds, Manchester and Birmingham arose, cities made up of factories whose great chimneys belched forth suffocating clouds of black smoke. And thousands who, like their forefathers before them, had been tenant farmers and craftsmen on the great feudal domains of the lords left the land and went to these cities.

A whole new strata of society came into being—factory workers. They were a landless people, huddling together in the most sordid of slums with disease and crime for companions. They worked—men, women and children as young as five years of age—for twelve, fourteen and sixteen hours a day, six days a week. And their wages were so low that they could barely keep body and soul together.

A new age had come into being. The Industrial Age. The wealthy English manufacturer of the 1830's, like all those who had gone before him, had no interest in politics, controlling only a few seats in the House of Commons, and no social conscience. He had only one object, and that was to make money. His factory buildings were deplorable places devoid of heat, proper lighting and sanitary conditions. The houses he rented to his workers were hovels hardly fit for animals. Indeed most of the barns in England were better structures.

Cheap labor meant more profits, and so the manufacturer paid his workers a pittance; they were actually industrial serfs. When they fell ill or grew too old to work, he cast them out like old clothes and hired younger and healthier people.

Why did the workers submit to such treatment? They did so in part because they had grown up in a society that believed in the caste system. They still accepted the outworn feudal concept that each man was born into a certain strata of society from which he could not escape; lucky ones were born into the nobility and were therefore entitled to enjoy wealth and serve as rulers; unlucky ones were born into the lower classes, whose destiny it was to serve the rich and noble and live in poverty.

Another reason why the workers submitted in dumb silence to the manufacturers was that they were uneducated. How could they be educated when there was no free education?

The condition of factory workers, of the poor everywhere, was deplorable. But the average Englishman of means enjoying three meals a day and the comforts of proper clothing and housing was not aware of its horror. And it was a young writer, not a social reformer, who was responsible for bringing these dreadful conditions to the attention of the English upper classes. His name was Charles Dickens.

During the year of 1837, the year when Victoria was crowned queen of England, a novel called *Oliver Twist* began to appear in monthly installments in a magazine called *Bentley's Miscellany*. Two years before, the twenty-six-year-old author of this work had attracted wide attention by the publication of his first book, *The Pickwick Papers*. In *The Pickwick Papers* he had displayed supreme powers as a humorist, and most people therefore expected that his second book would also be in this vein. But Dickens, who had known abject poverty in childhood and whose father had been in debtor's prison, understood how grim the situation was and had decided to expose it. He had therefore written a crusading novel, serious and moving. In it he showed clearly what poverty was like and how the Poor Law, which established workhouses and which had been enacted only a few years before, in 1834, was, as Dizzy said, a "disgrace" to the country.

*Oliver Twist* was read by a large public. People could

hardly wait for the next installment. In fact, on the day when a new issue was to come off the press the people in London waited in line to buy their copies.

Dickens had captured the English reading public as no author before him. Here was a story of hopeless poverty, cruelty and crime. It was immediate and vital. And all who read it realized it was true. Everyone in the land, no matter how rich and isolated he might be, now knew the truth.

The working class was slow to grumble. However, only a few months after Queen Victoria was crowned, things came to a head. Several bad harvests had reduced the farm workers to a desperate plight. Then a business depression occurred. Large factories shut down in more than a dozen cities. In Manchester alone 50,000 people were out of work. And since there were no provisions for relief, most of these people, farmers and factory workers alike, were on the verge of starvation.

There were riots, machine-smashings and, on farmlands, burning of haystacks.

A people's movement, called "The Chartists," sprang up, many of whom advocated violence. Among other things they demanded a share in the profits through higher wages, universal male suffrage and vote by ballot.

Others, led by a man called Cobden, formed an Anti-Corn Law Association, asking that the high duties on imported grain, which protected the powerful landowners and farmers who raised grain, be lowered so that the masses could have cheap bread.

The government was faced with insurrection. And there were few in Parliament who understood what had gone wrong—few except Disraeli. Through his years of intensive reading and study of great men, history and politics he had formed certain opinions which he now voiced with great passion.

He rose in Parliament, day after day, and spoke out frankly. Placing the blame squarely on the Whigs, he said that they, more than any other single group, persisted in clinging to outworn ideas and practices. He pointed out that the Whigs consistently refused to recognize the fact that the great mass of workers were people with intelligence and the ability to help rule themselves. He contended that the Whigs had denied these people the right to vote and the right to representation in Parliament. They had instead insisted that Parliament be controlled by a select group: lords, landowners and a handful of those who had enough money to pay rents above a stipulated sum. He accused the Whigs of having deliberately implanted in the minds of the uneducated masses the idea that only a select group in England, the upper class, had the right to rule. And he maintained that the result of such an attitude was that the country was run for the exclusive benefit of the upper class and with an inhuman disregard for the rights of the masses.

Having said what he thought of the Whigs, Disraeli now turned against his own party. He blamed the Tories for repeatedly supporting Whig measures and for a lack of vision and constructive action. He said that he would not support any government which did not at once introduce some measures to improve the conditions of the lower classes. And he sympathized openly with the Chartists in their demand for wider suffrage and a fair share of the profits of their labor.

Such frankness was, of course, not appreciated by Sir Robert Peel, the leader of the Tories, and Disraeli's political future was imperiled. However, he was not deterred and when the Whig government fell in 1841 and a general election was called, he decided to run as Tory candidate from Shrewsbury, a city about 135 miles northwest of London. He ran on the platform that if elected he would not sacrifice one class in the community to the benefit of another class. All would be treated equally.

Such words were almost revolutionary, and so the entrenched interests fought him with all the means in their power. They even resorted to accusing him of running for Parliament to escape prison, and they printed a long list of his unpaid debts.

But in spite of all their efforts Dizzy won. Writing with evident satisfaction to Sarah he said, "We had a sharp contest, but never for a moment doubtful. They did against me, and said against me, and wrote against me all they could find or invent; but I licked them."

The Tories had won a tremendous victory in the elections, and their leader, Robert Peel, became prime minister. Disraeli, who was very close to Peel and who had worked so hard for the party, naturally expected to receive a cabinet post or some other office of distinction in

Peel's government. But day after day passed and no word from Peel.

When the silence continued Disraeli became desperate. Could Peel seek such revenge for his having spoken the truth? He finally could bear it no longer and wrote Peel a letter.

He said that he had struggled for years against "a storm of political hate and malice" such as few men knew and that he had only withstood this onslaught because of the "conviction that the day would come when the foremost man of this country [Prime Minister Peel] would publicly testify that he had some respect for my ability and my character."

Disraeli was in fact so upset by Peel's slight that Mary Anne decided to intervene. Secretly she wrote to Peel reminding him of all the money she had given to the party in the past and begging him not to be cruel. "Do not destroy all his hopes," she pleaded, "and make him feel that his life has been a mistake."

But Peel was not moved.

# 7 YOUNG ENGLAND AND OLD IRELAND

POVERTY AND BREAD TURNED THE PARLIAMENTARY session of 1843 into a tense and difficult one. Disraeli was so deeply involved that he and Mary Anne seldom went out. He wrote to Sarah saying that they were unable to accept dinner invitations and that he dined instead "at the House of Commons, on a couple of mutton chops and cayenne pepper."

But complain as he did about his poor meals, he enjoyed every moment of the battle in which he found himself. And with his unorthodox ideas, he soon became the leader of a small group of young men, new Tory members of the Commons, who also expressed ideas different from those of the old and respected members. They were George Smythe, John Manners and Alexander

Baillie Cochrane, graduates of Eton and Cambridge; all were rich, the two first being the sons of noblemen, but their sympathies lay with the working people.

Like Disraeli they had great sympathy for labor and approved of measures that would relieve poverty, but they felt that the lords of England should rule, for they were the proper guardians of the people's happiness. It was the middle class, the new-rich, whom they disliked and distrusted. Their hope was to build a strong and enduring relationship between the peers of the land and the people.

As leader of "Young England," as this group came to be called, Disraeli sided with the prime minister on some measures, but on others he sounded a strong opposing voice. He questioned Prime Minister Peel on his foreign policy and his policy toward Ireland. The result was that "Young England" came forward as a small but strong opposition. This was a situation which Peel did not welcome, for Dizzy was the ablest speaker in the House, and so the breach which already existed between them was broadened.

Knowing this and fearing the consequences, Peel's sister wrote to Mary Anne saying that it would be nice if next time Disraeli met the prime minister he would shake hands. "They are both reserved men," she observed, "and one must make the first advance; the other would accept it most gladly."

But this suggestion was not followed. Disraeli was now labeled by his more conservative brother Tories as "impudent" and "shabby." Some went so far as to suggest that it would be best for Peel and the Tories if Disraeli "were driven into the open ranks of the enemies."

If Disraeli was becoming increasingly unpopular with some members of his party, his speeches, which were powerful in their logic and devastating in their sarcasm and ridicule, were making him extremely popular elsewhere. He was sought after more than any other Tory. Important people invited him to their social functions. And when, in the spring of 1844, he published a very fine new autobiographical novel called *Coningsby* explaining the political theories of "Young England," his fame skyrocketed.

*Coningsby*, which was also published in America, established Disraeli permanently as an author of importance, and the Parliamentary session of 1844 established him as the greatest speaker in England. His attacks against Prime Minister Peel's policies and his defense of those ideals in which he and "Young England" believed were so electrifying that whenever he rose to speak foes and friends alike hurried to their seats and a silence charged with expectation filled the chamber. Visitors jammed the gallery. And although his speeches were long —many lasted over three hours, and one lasted without interruption for five hours—no one ever left his bench to go home!

Dizzy had his own manner of speaking. He did not deliver a speech with the thundering voice of an orator. He started very quietly, in a clear voice, low and almost monotonous. He was calm, detached and very matter-of-fact. He added fact upon fact, allowing the material itself to build the weight of his message. He spoke without notes even though his speeches contained many dates, figures and other data. He recited all from memory. On one occasion he held a blank sheet of paper and pretended to look at it only to annoy Gladstone, the leader of the Liberal party, who could never speak without notes.

He restrained from gestures or other dramatic emphasis. His entire manner was one of comfort and ease. He kept his hands on his hips or hooked his thumbs into the armholes of his vest. And his face was placid, almost expressionless.

All this was part of a calculated effect. He was marking time. Finally, arriving at the place in his speech where he wanted to make a critical point, everything changed. His manner was no longer quiet, calm and detached. His voice suddenly sprang to life, becoming highly animated. His phrases were marked with precision; they were cutting and devastating. Sometimes he used bitter irony, sometimes sarcasm and sometimes ridicule. But whatever method he used it was always devastating and electrifying.

The House, held breathless, responded. Sometimes they roared with laughter, sometimes they gasped in surprise and shock, and sometimes they cheered and applauded. Dizzy pretended that he saw nothing and heard nothing. He stood waiting calmly without any expression, not even a smile on his face. He waited until the House was again quiet. Then he began once more in his quiet, calm, matter-of-fact manner with his voice clear but monotonous. Again he added fact upon fact, building into a fresh situation until he had another point to drive home with irony, precision or ridicule. And every point that he drove home was another nail in his enemy's coffin!

It was at about this time, 1844, that Disraeli helped put through some important labor and social reforms, the most important being the Ten Hours Factory Bill and a mining bill.

The Ten Hours Factory Bill was presented to Parliament by Lord Ashley. In most factories, as already noted, men, women and children were forced to work for twelve and sometimes fourteen and sixteen hours a day. Lord Ashley's bill asked for a ten-hour limit.

The bill was violently attacked by both landowners and factory owners and would have been defeated had Disraeli not come to the rescue. He asserted that labor had rights that "were as sacred as those of property," and he said that it was the duty of all statesmen to provide for "the social happiness of the millions."

After his Factory Bill was passed, Lord Ashley presented a coal mining bill. He felt that the mining of coal underground was not fit labor for women and young children. And with Disraeli's full support he got Parliament to prohibit the employment in coal mines of women and girls and of boys under thirteen.

This success was followed by still another social act. Lord Ashley's third bill established lodginghouses for those who were destitute.

Ireland had been under English domination since the twelfth century, and Disraeli felt that it was England's mismanagement of Ireland over this long period which had brought about the widespread discontent and deplorable state of affairs which existed in that poor country. He said that Ireland's misery was a blot on England's name. He felt that every effort should be made to change this dangerous situation. He said that the problem was so grave that all party lines must be abandoned. And so disregarding Prime Minister Peel and Tory policy toward Ireland, he raised his voice and used his eloquence on the "Irish question."

Dizzy had great courage and dared to say things that no other Englishman would say, things which expressed his honest opinion. "What is this Irish question?" he asked. "One says it is physical and another says it is spiritual. Now it is the absence of an aristocracy, then the absence of railroads. It is the Pope one day and potatoes the next."

Then he described Ireland as a place which was greatly overpopulated, without resources, without industry and completely dependent on agriculture. The population was half-starved. The rich Irish aristocrats lived abroad. English rule over Ireland was weak and indifferent. The Church of England was not the church of the people of Ireland. In all ways, temperamentally and spiritually, England and Ireland were at opposite poles.

"What is the remedy?" he asked. "Is it revolution?" No. Revolution he felt must be avoided at all costs.

Then, he reasoned, if England were the chief cause of misery in Ireland, it was the duty of the English Parliament to devise a just plan for the relief of Ireland. He concluded by saying that he would support any party that put forward such a bill, even though he might have to explain his stand to his constituency and later resign from the House of Commons.

He was outspoken. He was bold. He was firm. And following his suggestion many measures were proposed and tried. But the differences were too great and the solutions presented were too weak. And so in spite of his efforts, a half-century later revolution came to Ireland.

# 8 TWO NATIONS

◆◆◆◆◆◆◆◆◆◆◆◆◆◆◆◆◆◆◆◆◆◆◆◆◆◆◆◆◆◆◆◆◆◆◆◆◆◆◆◆◆◆◆

WHEN THE PARLIAMENTARY SESSION OF 1844 CAME to a close, Disraeli, accompanied by Mary Anne, traveled through England, visiting farmers, laborers and factory workers. Dizzy wanted to see at first hand everything for which he was fighting. And what he saw was frightening.

The idea came to him that the best way to bring these shocking conditions to the attention of the English upper classes was by depicting them in a novel. In *Oliver Twist* Dickens had focused attention on the problem of city slums. He would write a novel depicting the deplorable conditions which existed in England's villages, farms and industrial towns.

He planned a novel entirely different from all those he had formerly written, different even from *Coningsby*.

This new book would not be autobiographical. It would deal only with the English people and their problems. It would be a serious work devoid of his usual wit and epigrams. The material would be dramatic and tragic. He would depict the struggle for existence, as he saw it: raw, brutal and unjust. The struggle would be between the rich and the poor.

Disraeli called his new novel *Sybil, or The Two Nations*.

*Sybil* was a shocking novel: every page was drawn from life. Yet it concluded with a ray of hope. Hope for the future, Dizzy felt, lay with the young people of England who were informed and aware of social injustice.

"We live in an age," he wrote, "when to be young and to be indifferent can be no longer synonymous. We must prepare for the coming hour. The claims of the Future are represented by the suffering millions: and the Youth of the Nation are the Trustees of Prosperity."

Once more Dizzy had a novel that attracted a wide public and became the talk of London. And while it was totally different from his other works and lacked the artistic qualities of a book by Dickens, still it served in a number of ways. It brought attention to a condition that was evil. It showed exactly what Dizzy thought and where he stood as a public servant and humanitarian. And it announced that there was work to be done and that the future depended upon "Young England."

This was the immediate effect of *Sybil*. But in a short time its message spread, and it influenced the social development of the rest of the Western world. Now, after a full century, *Sybil* is recognized as the very first novel in all literature to deal with the struggle between rich and poor—the very first "labor novel."

The deplorable conditions pictured in *Sybil* did not improve immediately. In fact they became worse. Much worse. In 1845, the very year in which *Sybil* was published, a great tragedy struck the British Isles. It became known in history as the Irish Potato Famine.

During that year a blight attacked the potatoes in Ireland, ruining more than half the crops. Since most of the people of Ireland depended for food upon potatoes rather than bread, a famine resulted which was one of the most terrible in all history. Whole families wandered the roads seeking food. One by one they dropped dead, and their bodies were left unburied. Others sat hopelessly in their cottages waiting for death.

During the five years the famine lasted, one million Irish people starved to death. Times were so bad that all those who could migrated to foreign lands. It is estimated that in the ten years following the onset of the famine one million people emigrated from Ireland, many of them to America.

Ireland was the first country to be stricken, but others were soon to suffer. The potato blight spread to England and then to Scotland, increasing the misery in both these countries. From there it spread to Belgium, Holland, Sweden and Denmark.

The people of these lands suffered, but not so much

as the people of the British Isles, especially Ireland, for their governments immediately imported wheat, thereby substituting bread for potatoes. England, however, could not do this because of the Corn Laws. If she had imported foreign grain, its cost would have been so high that the poor could not have bought the bread into which it was made!

And so the tragic conflict between the rich and poor as depicted by Disraeli in *Sybil* was only intensified. The queen's husband, Prince Albert, wrote to his brother, "The potato crops have turned out very badly and will lead to the greatest political complications—it is impossible to argue with famished people."

Disraeli expressed it in another way. "These rotted potatoes," he said, "are going to change the world."

The necessity of the time required immediate action. A movement headed by Prime Minister Peel and endorsed by the queen was at once started in Parliament to repeal the Corn Laws. But this solution was weighted with dangers.

Farsighted men such as Disraeli knew that if the Corn Laws were repealed and cheap foreign grain flooded the British Isles, English agriculture would be dealt a death blow, manufacturing would spread and England would become a purely industrial country. Besides, the Irish were so desperately poor that even with cheap grain they would still not have money enough to buy bread. England would therefore be running a very serious risk without solving its main problem, the relief of the starving Irish.

Disraeli presented his view in Parliament, but Peel could not be moved. Peel completely abandoned Tory policy and his campaign promises to "protect" English landowners and farmers and became an advocate of "free trade," a policy which benefited only the manufacturers. And so Disraeli launched a vehement attack against Peel, the head of his own party.

The question was so important that it cut across party lines; Disraeli headed a "Protectionist" opposition made up not only of "Young England" but of thinking men from both the Tories and the Whigs, while Peel was supported by the hard core of both of these same parties, all "Free Traders."

The debates were long and fierce. They sometimes lasted until four or five in the morning. But when Dizzy returned home at the point of exhaustion, he found comfort and peace. Mary Anne was waiting for him. Fires were burning in the grates. Every room was bright with lights—Dizzy loved plenty of light—and his dinner was ready and hot.

On other nights Mary Anne wrapped herself in a warm cloak and drove down to Parliament in her carriage. There at the gate she waited through the night with a tray of cold supper on the seat beside her.

Dizzy's attacks against the repeal of the Corn Laws and Prime Minister Peel were violent and brilliant. Every seat was taken. No one would miss a word of what he said. But Peel and his supporters were powerful enough to bring his bill to a vote three successive times.

With each vote Peel gained greater support. In the end his policy won out. The Corn Laws were repealed. But Dizzy had exposed Peel so completely as a person and a politician that in spite of his triumph, Peel was forced to resign as prime minister.

# 9 A LONESOME BATTLE

✦✦✦✦✦✦✦✦✦✦✦✦✦✦✦✦✦✦✦✦✦✦✦✦✦✦✦✦✦✦✦✦✦✦

DISRAELI EMERGED FROM HIS DEBATES WITH PEEL AS one of the most important political figures in England and as head of a large opposition party made up of all those who had supported him and called the Conservative party.

He had risen to power through his tremendous ability and brilliance and his understanding of changing times. But because Dizzy championed the poor and openly defended factory workers, farm laborers and other downtrodden groups, it must not be assumed that he was a liberal. He had a deep sense of justice, and it was justice rather than liberalism that moved him to defend those who were defenseless. He advocated only moderate reforms. Those who believed in extreme reforms were known as Liberals and for many years had as a leader the statesman William Gladstone.

Disraeli believed in monarchy. He believed that "gentlemen" should be the rulers of England. He supported the aristocracy, asking only that these lords and squires treat their workers and tenants with the kind of consideration and decency which he imagined had been displayed in olden days.

His friends were people of high station. Most of them were titled and rich. And so, oddly enough, while defending the poor, he became the spokesman of a class: the landed gentlemen, the lords of the manor. And yet he himself had no land and no manor.

To have a fine estate in the country now became the desire of his heart. And what he desired he usually achieved.

Disraeli's father, Isaac D'Israeli, to whom he was ever devoted, was now old. He lived on his Brandenham estate, surrounded by a vast library. But he could no longer read the books he loved so much. He had been blind for the last ten years.

Isaac D'Israeli was very proud of Benjamin, and knowing of his heart's desire, he one day informed him that a very fine estate close to Brandenham, called Hughenden Manor, was for sale. It was a most unusual estate dating from the days of Queen Elizabeth, and he felt it was exactly right for Benjamin and Mary Anne. It consisted of 750 acres, lawns, meadows, woods, a stream, fine old trees, a great manor house, long avenues of beeches and a park in which was located a little church, a vicarage and cottages for the workers. Besides, it was in Buckinghamshire and Dizzy had just been elected to Parliament from this district, a post which he was to hold for many years to come. The only trouble was the price. It was worth 35,000 pounds, or 175,000 dollars.

Isaac D'Israeli knew that he did not have much longer to live, and to secure such a wonderful place for Benjamin he proposed to give him his inheritance at once, 10,000 pounds. It was a very nice sum, but unfortunately hardly enough.

However, Dizzy, who was fond of saying, "I play for high stakes," accepted the 10,000 pounds. He used it for a down payment, feeling certain that he could raise the additional 25,000 pounds.

Mary Anne could not help him, for she had just paid 13,000 pounds on his debts. Nevertheless toward the end of the year his dream came true. A rich friend, Lord George Bentinck, lent him the necessary balance.

As soon as the papers were signed, Dizzy wrote to Mary Anne, who was in London, "You are now the Lady of Hughenden."

Disraeli's gentle mother died on April 21, 1847, at the age of seventy-one. Nine months later on January 19, 1848, his father died. He was eighty-one years old.

The death of his parents, especially that of his father, grieved Disraeli greatly. But the time he spent at Hughenden Manor helped heal his sorrow.

He and Mary Anne spent many hours exploring their large estate. He walked and Mary Anne rode alongside him in a little pony cart. He was now forty-four and she was fifty-six. In London he wore somber clothes befitting his position in Parliament, but in the country he began wearing his beloved fancy and colorful waistcoats!

Dizzy had a great love of nature—the woods, the fresh yellow-green of spring as well as the russet of fall, the fields on which he had a fine herd of cows, the broad lawns. But above all he loved the trees. These he loved so passionately that he would not allow a single one to be cut down.

And it was no passing fancy. Disraeli's great love of trees was with him to his last day. He even remembered the trees at Hughenden in his will, leaving strict orders that none should be cut. He once wrote, "I have a passion for trees. . . . When I come down to Hughenden I pass the first week in sauntering about my park and examining all the trees. . . ." At another time he noted, "A forest is like an ocean, monotonous only to the ignorant. It is a life of ceaseless variety."

Dizzy and Mary Anne were now "lord" and "lady" of a manor. Hughenden became their home. They fitted into this baronial estate with such ease that it seemed they had always been there. They made improvements. They cut new paths through the woods and across the meadows, placed benches under shady trees and repaired the barns and workers' cottages. And they added strutting peacocks to the terraces. "You cannot have terraces without peacocks," Dizzy explained.

Lord George Bentinck, who had advanced the 25,000 pounds that enabled Dizzy to buy Hughenden, was the son of the Duke of Portland. The duke had the distinction of being the first governor-general of India. He was a public-spirited person, but his son, George, while a member of Parliament, had only a mild interest in politics. His true love, his passion, was horses. He had a fine stable and was a lover of racing. He often attended sessions in a white greatcoat which hid his red hunting coat.

In Parliament he was always silent. He attended sessions for many years without ever voicing an opinion. However, when Prime Minister Peel and Disraeli became involved in the conflict over the repeal of the Corn Laws, his whole attitude changed. He suddenly became intensely interested, and although he was a Whig, he joined Disraeli's opposition, becoming one of his most ardent and outspoken supporters. His interest was so intense that he gave up horse racing and sold his entire stable. And alas, in the season which followed, one of the horses he had sold won the Derby!

It was shortly after the fall of Peel that Dizzy waged a campaign in the House of Commons which proved to be very unpopular with everyone, even the members of his own party. In this battle Dizzy risked his political future. Everyone was against him. Only Bentinck supported him.

The bill which precipitated this sudden change in Disraeli's fortunes and popularity was one which had been suggested by the new prime minister, John Russell, providing for the removal of civil and political restrictions against Jews. The reason that this question had come to the fore was that Baron Lionel Rothschild had just been elected to the House of Commons by the City of London, a district in London. The baron was the head of the London branch of the famous international banking house, the House of Rothschild, which had served England long and faithfully. It was the House of Rothschild which had lent England money to fight Napoleon.

Lionel Rothschild's knowledge of finance and international trade would be invaluable to the legislators in Parliament. However, he could not take his seat because, as a Jew, he could not take the oath of office which required him to swear "on the true faith of a Christian."

This oath of office had been administered for centuries, and almost all the members of Parliament were against having it changed. They were opposed for two reasons: some hated to see an ancient tradition altered, but most objected because they were basically unjust and unreasonable men and were deeply prejudiced against Jews and wanted to keep them out of Parliament.

Disraeli, who had been baptized when thirteen, had readily taken the "Christian" oath. But he firmly believed that every Englishman should have the same rights under the constitution whether he was an atheist, a Christian, a Jew, a Mohammedan or a member of any other religious group. In other words, Disraeli believed in religious freedom and wanted to see an end to prejudice.

And so he spoke out boldly. He said that the history of the Jews was an integral part of Christianity. He reminded his listeners that not alone was Jesus a Jew but so too were the Apostles and all the early Christians. Even the "throne of Rome" had been established by a Jew. "Where is your Christianity if you do not believe in their Judaism?" And he asked if England was not clinging to the intolerance of the Middle Ages.

The members of the House were so disturbed and angered by the obvious truths with which he confronted them that they interrupted him over and over again. But he did not let their antagonism alter his course, and he concluded his long speech with the words, "I cannot sit in this House with any misconception of my opinion on this subject. . . . Yes, it is as a Christian that I will not take upon me the awful responsibility of excluding from the legislature those who are of the religion in the bosom of which my Lord and Savior was born."

Disraeli's courageous and dramatic speech was over. This time he received no applause. There was only cold silence.

The bill was lost, but Disraeli was not defeated. He determined to continue the fight until victory was achieved, and in his spare time he wrote a novel called *Tancred* giving his views on religion. Together with *Coningsby* and *Sybil, Tancred* completed a trilogy on politics, social conditions and religion.

Publishing such a book as *Tancred* was a very courageous thing to do considering how tense people were about religion and how much prejudice existed in England at the time. His only real supporter was George Bentinck, but he was soon to lose even him. Walking one day through the woods on his father's estate, George Bentinck dropped dead, his heart strained from the work he had done with Dizzy in Parliament.

Disraeli was deeply grieved. "It is the greatest sorrow I have ever experienced," he wrote to Bentinck's brother. "A peculiar and unparalleled spirit has departed. . . . I can neither offer, nor receive, consolation."

So deep was the prejudice of the members of Parliament that the battle over the "Christian" oath continued, off and on, for ten long years. For ten long years, Disraeli fought on alone, even though he knew that he might be sealing his political doom and destroying the dream which he had nurtured since earliest childhood of becoming prime minister.

Then at last in 1858 he won. And from that day on Jews in England enjoyed equal rights with all other English citizens. They could attend universities, practice law, hold civil appointments and serve as members of Parliament.

# 10 WHO? WHO?

◆◆◆◆◆◆◆◆◆◆◆◆◆◆◆◆◆◆◆◆◆◆◆◆◆◆◆◆◆◆◆◆◆◆◆◆◆◆◆◆◆◆◆◆◆

ON A BRIGHT MORNING IN 1850, FOLLOWING A LONG
and tiring night session in the House, Mary Anne persuaded Dizzy to take a carriage drive with her through
Regent's Park. As they were rolling along talking happily together, two strangers on horseback stopped their
carriage and reported that Sir Robert Peel had been
thrown by his horse and carried home in a dangerous
condition. The next day he died.

Disraeli was sincerely grieved by Peel's untimely
death, even though they had become political enemies.
Nevertheless, with Peel gone his position in Parliament
became still stronger. When Prime Minister John Russell
fell in 1851 and the queen summoned the leader of the
House and member of the Conservative party, Lord

Stanley, to form a new government, it appeared as though Disraeli would advance one step closer to his goal of becoming prime minister.

The queen asked Lord Stanley whom he intended to have as leader of the House of Commons, and he said, "Disraeli."

The queen frowned and answered, "I do not approve of Mr. Disraeli. I do not approve of his conduct to Sir Robert Peel, and Sir Robert's death does not tend to lessen that feeling."

However, thinking of how Disraeli had risen to his high position with neither birth nor influence to help him, Lord Stanley replied, "Madam, Mr. Disraeli has had to make his position, and men who make their positions will say and do things which are not necessary to those for whom positions are provided."

The queen understood. "That is true," she said, and she agreed to Lord Stanley's choice of Disraeli. "All I can now hope is that, having attained this great position, he will be temperate. I accept Mr. Disraeli on your guarantee."

However, Lord Stanley was unable to form a government. He was a stanch "Protectionist" believing, like Disraeli, in high tariffs to protect British agriculture as well as industry, and he was unable to win over Peel's followers, who believed just as stanchly in "Free Trade," or no tariffs.

Confonted with this serious setback, Dizzy, who was a realist, drew up a plan to win over the followers of the late Peel. He would show both these men, and the members of his own party, that there were other problems besides protection and free trade. He would raise their sights from local English problems to problems concerning the Empire. So he presented a program to reform Parliament. He proposed that the colonies be given a share in the administration of the Empire.

Stanley, or Lord Derby, as he was now called, did not think much of Disraeli's scheme. Nevertheless it worked. He was now able to rally the necessary support in Parliament, and the queen called him to Buckingham Palace to ask him to form a new government.

Leaving the palace and driving directly to Dizzy's house in Park Lane, he announced, "You will be the chancellor of the exchequer." This meant that Disraeli would be head of the treasury and have charge of all money collected by the revenue department. He would make up the annual government budget and disperse all funds for civilian and military needs.

Dizzy protested that he knew nothing about finance— a rather obvious fact since he was still deeply in debt.

But Lord Derby could not be influenced. The next day the ministry, or cabinet, was formed. Since the Conservatives had very few members who had served in other ministries, all its members but three were "unknowns." In fact they were so little known that when the list of names was read to the Duke of Wellington, who was now very old and deaf, he kept asking, "Who? Who?"

The newspapers printed this story and so Lord Derby's cabinet became known as the "Who Who Cabinet."

With the change in government Dizzy was elevated to another post beside that of chancellor of the exchequer. He inherited the position of leader of the House from Lord Derby, who was now prime minister. As such it was his duty to send the queen each day a brief summary of the debates.

These reports had always been written in a formal manner. But now with the advent of Disraeli their tone changed. They were informal and rather personal. Queen Victoria was a little disturbed by the whole thing. She remarked that Mr. Disraeli's reports read like his novels. However, since they were always deeply respectful to her, she got to like them.

Neither Queen Victoria nor Prince Albert at first liked "the Jew," as Prince Albert, indulging in prejudice, called Disraeli in private. They had followed his rise very closely and were rather critical of his frankness and ambition. But after his first few visits with them, they changed their minds. Like so many others before them, they found him not only witty and charming but brilliant and filled with good sense.

For his part, Dizzy found the queen most gracious. His affection for her was genuine. He had, in fact, liked her from the very first moment when he saw her as a young girl during the coronation ceremonies in Westminster Abbey.

As for Prince Albert, Dizzy soon discovered that he

liked him too. Writing to Sarah, he said, "On Sunday I was two hours with the prince, a very gracious and interesting audience. He has great abilities and wonderful knowledge—I think him the best educated man I ever met. . . ."

The relations between Disraeli and the queen and her prince became most cordial, but unfortunately the government which had brought them together lasted only ten months. Then the political applecart was upset.

The reason for this quick change of government was Disraeli himself. Ten months of Disraeli as leader of the House was more than the leaders of the other political factions could stand. They were jealous of him. They could not tolerate the fact that this man, who came from Jewish parentage and had no formal schooling, had by his intelligence and ability alone risen to a position which they who had titles, birth, money and the finest educations were unable to achieve. And so when, as minister of the exchequer, he presented his budget they formed a coalition and attacked him with every means at their disposal.

Disraeli was not fully recovered from influenza when he came into the House to answer his critics. He spoke for five and a half hours, during which time he was repeatedly interrupted. When he finished he was on the verge of collapse.

Then for a whole week he was subjected to the most offensive treatment. He was baited, mocked, taunted, derided and jeered at, especially by those members of the

House who had been supporters of Sir Robert Peel. But since he had a nature which was not easily disturbed by adversity, he stood up under the barrage.

After the opposition had said all it could think of, he again rose to speak. He understood fully why he was being hounded. But his defense fell upon deaf ears. The vote was against him and his party.

In defeat, Disraeli was always generous and gracious, and this time was no exception.

Overlooking the cruel treatment he had received, he thanked the House for its tolerance and attention, adding that he hoped that in the heat of his arguments he had not said anything offensive to anyone. That very night he wrote farewell notes to both Queen Victoria and Prince Albert.

He wrote to the prince saying that he would always remember him with admiration. To the queen, who was very disappointed at losing him, he said that he was deeply grateful for all the kindness she had bestowed upon him. She could count on his devotion and loyalty.

The grace and courtesy of these farewells, coming as they did at the end of such a bitter fight and in the face of such a humiliating defeat, have probably never been equaled.

# 11 THE OLD LADY OF TORQUAY

✧✧✧✧✧✧✧✧✧✧✧✧✧✧✧✧✧✧✧✧✧✧✧✧✧✧✧✧✧✧✧✧✧✧✧✧✧

THE COALITION WHICH HAD DEFEATED DISRAELI'S Conservative party now came into power. Earl Aberdeen, a Tory, became prime minister, and the cabinet posts were allotted to leaders of the other factions. Palmerston, a Whig, became minister of the home office, and Gladstone, a Liberal, took over Disraeli's post of minister of the exchequer.

The queen did not care for Mr. Gladstone. He was totally devoid of humor, and his liberal ideas were frightening. He was also extremely religious. He embarrassed everyone at the luncheon and dinner table by mumbling endless prayers over his food. The queen longed for Disraeli. He was so different, so refreshing.

Dizzy explained it by saying, "Gladstone treats the

queen as though she were an institution. I treat her as a woman."

Besides he had the grace to be respectful and courteous. When dealing with the queen he followed a simple rule. "I never deny. I never contradict. I sometimes forget."

Queen Victoria was, however, not the only lady to become deeply attached to Disraeli at this time. He loved the company of women and seemed to know exactly what to say to them and how to treat them. Besides Mary Anne, Sarah and the queen there were many others who thought of him with fondness. One of these was a certain rich widow, Mrs. Brydges Willyams, who lived in Torquay on the southern coast of England.

Mrs. Willyams, like many others all over Britain, followed Disraeli's career with interest and often wrote him commenting on his speeches and books. She was particularly attracted to him because of his long battle in Parliament to change the "Christian" oath. Like Disraeli, she was of Spanish Jewish origin, being descended from the old and distinguished Mendez da Costa family, a branch of the House of Lara. And she firmly believed that she and he were related because, according to her records, the Israeli family was a branch of the House of Lara.

Disraeli, who received a great of fan mail, did not personally answer any of Mrs. Willyam's letters until the year of 1851 when she was over seventy years of age. In fact, before then, he used to joke about her, asking his friends, "Do any of you know an old madwoman at Torquay?" And he only troubled to answer her at that time because she had written asking that he act as an executor of her will. He replied that he and Mary Anne were planning to be close to Torquay in the autumn and that they would visit her at her home, Mount Braddon, to discuss the problem.

This first meeting was apparently a very pleasant one, for not only did Disraeli become an executor of Mrs. Willyam's will but both he and Mary Anne became her closest friends. For the remaining twelve years of her life, the Disraelis spent two weeks each year in Torquay. And a daily correspondence was kept up between Hughenden Manor and Mount Braddon.

She contributed money to his campaigns and asked his advice on legal matters. She followed with the greatest interest every detail concerning the restoration of Hughenden Manor to what it had been in the days of the Stuarts. She was awaiting photographs which Dizzy had had made expressly for her of the house and its terraces and gardens, when she died.

Her devotion to Dizzy had been complete. In her will she bequeathed him a sum equal to $150,000, which he used to pay off his enormous debts. And so for the first time in over thirty years, for the first time since he was young and had borrowed to gamble with South American stocks, he was almost free of debt.

Within a year of assuming power, Prime Minister Aberdeen's coalition government drifted into a war with Russia. Dreaming of conquest and a Mediterranean seaport, Czar Nicholas invaded that part of the Turkish Empire which is now Romania. France and England immediately sent their fleets and armed forces to Constantinople to support Turkey. The Crimean War was on, a war remembered today mainly because of Florence Nightingale and Tennyson's poem, *The Charge of the Light Brigade.*

Disraeli, of course, gave his full support to the coalition government in its war against Russia. But the situation in the Crimea, a large Russian peninsula jutting out into the Black Sea, where the war was being fought, went from bad to worse. While the allies won several battles, by the end of 1854 the coalition government had become very unpopular. Shortly thereafter it fell, and the queen again summoned Lord Derby, Disraeli's closest political ally, to form a government.

Lord Derby declined the queen's offer to become prime minister, saying that Viscount Palmerston, a Liberal, was far better equipped to lead the country during these difficult times. And so although no one knew it at the time, Disraeli at fifty years of age, was thereby doomed to spend sixteen more long years in politics before being elevated to the position of prime minister.

With the fall of Sevastopol in September 1855 the Crimean War had actually come to an end. But England had gone war crazy, and Palmerston wanted to start another campaign to drive the Russians out of the Crimea. Disraeli objected. He maintained that English and French occupation of the Crimea would certainly lead to serious trouble with Russia at some later date, and he exerted every effort to bring about a saner view of the situation. He was finally able to convince Palmerston to abandon his mad idea, and the Treaty of Paris was signed in the spring of 1856. It was a very reasonable treaty: Russia was simply to withdraw her troops from Turkish territory in the Balkans.

Another problem which occupied Disraeli at this period concerned the United States. There was considerable objection in England to America's continued westward expansion; people were fearful that she might never stop annexing new lands. Disraeli disagreed and defended the United States. He said that United States expansion was beneficial to England; as the United States annexed wild areas and developed them, it indirectly contributed to England's wealth by stimulating general growth and trade.

A third question on which Disraeli maintained a different opinion from that held by the mass of the people and members of Parliament was India. And, as always, he was courageous and frank in presenting his view.

There had been a revolt in India, the Indian Mutiny. Some atrocities against English men, women and children had occurred. Luckily they were limited in number;

but in England rumors were rife, and the people cried for revenge, as did many of their leaders. Disraeli alone took an opposite stand.

He recommended that the government refrain from revenge. He advised the government to resort instead to justice and mercy—"justice the most severe and mercy the most indulgent."

He went still further; he touched at the root of all the trouble—the East India Company. He said that the East India Company, which had been running India for the past 100 years as a private business and dividing its incredible wealth among its stockholders, was the cause of all the trouble. He accused the East India Company of being excessively greedy and completely insensible to Indian customs, castes and religious beliefs. This attitude, he maintained, was creating fanatical hatred against England. He recommended that India be taken away from the East India Company and transferred to the English government.

Disraeli's advice fell upon deaf ears. But he was not to be blocked, and his chance came the following year when Lord Derby once more became prime minister and he minister of the exchequer.

Disraeli immediately brought up the India question in Parliament. He engaged in a whole series of debates with those who opposed him, men who in some cases had personal interests in the East India Company.

The battle was so fierce that Dizzy was in danger of losing his seat. But he did not care. He fought as always for what he felt was best for England. And in the end he won; India was transferred from the East India Company to the crown.

The interest which Disraeli, singlehandedly, had aroused in this grave question was such that on the day of his victory as he left Parliament he was cheered by crowds in the street.

Disraeli now turned his attention to a very different problem. He turned from India to sewage.

For some time he had been distressed by bad odors coming from the Thames on hot summer days. Looking into the matter, he discovered that the river was nothing more than an open drain. It served as an important part of London's sewage system. This, naturally created a very unhealthy condition, one which endangered the people's lives.

His bill provided for a proper drainage system for London. In this way the historic Thames would be made pure and the people spared the danger of pestilence.

When the bill was passed, Disraeli was very pleased. He said, "A policy that diminishes the death rate of a nation is an important accomplishment."

When Parliament was in session, Dizzy never missed a single day. He kept track of every debate and informed himself on every bill. This, added to his speeches, naturally created a great deal of work. And so when a season of nerve-racking sessions drew to a close, he always needed a rest.

Mary Anne, therefore, always tried to plan some diversion for the summer. Whenever possible she took him to Europe. They would rest for several weeks at some spa and then go to Paris, where they had many good friends including the emperor of France, Napoleon III, and the Empress Eugenie.

However, some summers, as a matter of politics and courtesy, they had to make a tour of the country houses of Dizzy's colleagues in Parliament.

Dizzy was always miserable visiting these homes. He did not care for his hosts and their friends. He always hoped he would find someone of real interest, but he was always disappointed. He was bored by their talk and by their pleasures. He disliked shooting game birds and hunting frightened foxes. At one country estate he saw, to his disgust, 1,200 birds slaughtered in one day. He has recorded, "the sky was darkened with their up-rushing and the whir of wings was like the roar of the sea."

Dizzy did not enjoy these visits. "I detest society really," he said, "for I never enter it without my feelings being hurt."

But Mary Anne in her lighthearted way expressed it differently. She told a friend, "Whenever we go to a country house the same thing happens; Dizzy is not only bored, and has constant ennui, but he takes to eating as a resource; he eats at breakfast, luncheon and dinner; the result is, by the end of the third day he becomes dreadfully bilious, and we have to come away."

# 12 PRIME MINISTER DISRAELI

◆◇◆◇◆◇◆◇◆◇◆◇◆◇◆◇◆◇◆◇◆◇◆◇◆◇◆◇◆◇◆◇◆◇◆◇◆◇◆◇◆◇◆

QUEEN VICTORIA WAS VERY PLEASED TO HAVE DIZZY
back as minister of the exchequer. She delighted in his
reports and visits. But again her pleasure was to be short-
lived. And this time, too, it was jealousy of Disraeli that
brought about the fall of Prime Minister Derby's government.

Dizzy had never been satisfied with the Reform Bill of
1832, which had extended the vote and reapportioned
representation. He did not feel that it had gone far
enough and he now introduced a new reform bill to extend the franchise still further. It was a good bill even
though it still limited the vote; Disraeli did not believe in
universal suffrage even for men. It favored no particular
class and yet made it possible for every important ele-
ment in the society to be adequately represented.

The Whigs, who prided themselves on being a party of reform, recognized its virtues but decided to kill it. They were determined to rob Disraeli, whose great intelligence and brilliance was always eclipsing them, of whatever popularity its success would have brought him.

The campaign the Whigs waged against Disraeli's reform bill was completely insincere and shabby. Yet they won out. They defeated the reform bill and thereby brought about the fall of Derby's government. But they were unable to muster enough strength in Parliament to form a new government, and so Palmerston, the Liberal, took over once more.

It had been a bitter defeat for Disraeli. But its sting was surpassed by a personal sorrow which visited him at the same time. His beloved sister, Sarah, she with whom he had shared all his joys and sorrows, died that same winter. In a letter written at that sad time he called her, "My first and ever faithful friend."

Seven more years of waiting now lay ahead, years during which Disraeli again served as leader of the opposition. Since few serious internal problems arose, his chief criticism centered on the foreign policy of Palmerston's government.

It was a period of social and political upheaval on the continent and in the United States. The unpopular king of Greece was deposed and a Danish prince was chosen to fill his place. The Italian states were consolidated into one nation by Garibaldi. And in the United States the Civil War broke out.

The American Civil War had a direct effect on England because the Union blockade prevented cotton from the Confederate States from reaching the English cotton mills. Many of these mills were forced to shut down for the full duration of the war. The populations of whole cities were starving.

But cotton was not the only tie which bound England to the South. A land such as England, traditionally ruled by an aristocracy, naturally had a great sympathy for the aristocratic southern states. And so certain southerners made propaganda in England trying to win the open approval of the English government. They even published a weekly periodical in London.

Dizzy sensed the great danger to England which lay in this Confederate propaganda, and he warned Palmerston's government to beware. He said that under no circumstances should England take sides in the American conflict.

He was an enemy of revolution and civil strife even when the results were noble—he was the only man of importance in England who refused to see Garibaldi when he visited London in 1864. His sympathies were definitely on the side of the Union and the established government of the United States.

His words in the House of Commons were forceful and convincing. "When I consider the great difficulties which the statesmen of North America have to encounter," he said, "when I consider what I call the awful emergency which they have been summoned suddenly to meet, and which they have met manfully and courageously, I think it becomes England, in dealing with the Government of the United States, to extend to all . . . a generous interpretation. . . ."

And so it was largely because of Dizzy's efforts that England did not become involved in the American Civil War. Not only did his wisdom prevail at this time, but he was one of the very few who foretold the future. He predicted that once the Civil War was finished and order was restored, the United States would grow into one of the most important of all world powers.

During this period, Dizzy's role as leader of the opposition was a rather dreary one. However, its dullness was brightened by his growing friendship with Queen Victoria.

In the same year that the Civil War broke out in the United States, the queen invited Dizzy and Mary Anne to stay with her and her family at Windsor Castle. Their friendship was further strengthened at the end of that same year when the prince consort died of a respiratory infection after only a few days' illness.

Poor Queen Victoria was desolate. She loved the prince dearly. He had been completely devoted to her and their children. And he had always helped her in the responsible task of governing the nation. He had, in fact, been so interested and active that Dizzy, who thought very highly of his ability, felt he had been the "ruler." "We have buried our sovereign," Dizzy said to an ambassador. "This German prince has governed England for twenty-one years with wisdom and energy. . . ."

However, the queen knew that the people of England did not feel the way Dizzy did. She knew that the public had never liked her German prince. Sometimes when her carriage passed through the streets and parks she had noticed people turning their backs upon her.

Because of the bitterness which this brought to her heart, Queen Victoria appreciated all the more the glowing tribute which Dizzy paid to the late prince in the House of Commons. More than once she was heard to say that Mr. Disraeli was the only person who truly appreciated Prince Albert. And in gratitude she sent Dizzy engravings of herself and the prince.

When, a short time later, Dizzy proposed to the House that a sum of money be appropriated for the erection of a monument to Prince Albert, Victoria's affection for Mr. Disraeli grew stronger still. Moved by his generous act, Victoria sent him her personal copy of the prince's speeches and a letter expressing her deep gratification at the tribute he paid to her "adored, beloved and great husband."

This was the final act binding two sympathetic souls together. From that moment on Victoria and Disraeli were joined by a friendship which nothing could rip asunder.

A year later when Victoria's eldest son Edward, Prince of Wales, was to marry Princess Alexandra of Denmark, it was discovered that the guest list was too long. All the royalty of England and Europe, together with the cabinet ministers, ambassadors and other high officials could not possibly be crowded into St. George's Chapel at Windsor Castle. When the list had been pruned down considerably, there were four seats left over. The queen had no hesitation. She ordered that two of these should go to Mr. Disraeli and his wife.

Disraeli's friendship with Queen Victoria was very pleasant, but there were other social engagements which were not to his liking but to which he had to give his time—visiting country houses. And so in the late summer of 1865 he and Mary Anne started out on another round of such visits.

During their stay at one great house, Disraeli met a young man named Montagu Corry. He was not much taken with the grave manner of the youth, not knowing that thus had Corry tried to impress the great statesman.

One rainy afternoon, the young ladies of the house got hold of Monty and, knowing his talents, begged him to dance and sing some funny songs for them. Dizzy, in an adjoining room, was attracted by the noise and coming quietly to the door saw the young man overflowing with fun and good will. He liked this Monty Corry.

That evening after supper he said to him, "I think you must be my impresario."

In this way did Monty Corry become Disraeli's private secretary and, in time, his most intimate friend. He proved to be completely devoted to Dizzy and remained at his side until the very last day of his life.

In 1866, after seven long years of waiting, Lord Derby was called to Buckingham Palace by the queen for a third time. And as before Derby chose Disraeli to serve as minister of the exchequer in his cabinet.

The queen was very happy to welcome Dizzy back into her government once more, but secretly she wished that he and not Lord Derby were going to serve her as prime minister. This was, of course, also Disraeli's desire. He had waited and served a long time—a very long time. He was now sixty-two years old. He would wait a little longer and then perhaps . . .

But there was no time to dream of happier days to come or to brood over disappointments. Demands for a reform bill, such as the one Disraeli had proposed seven years before and which the Whigs had killed, were being loudly voiced. In fact, just a few weeks after Lord Derby became prime minister, riots broke out in Hyde Park. So Disraeli set to work at once to draw up a new proposal, one which he hoped would win the approval of all.

To accomplish this he had to compromise. Still he drew up a fine bill which at one stroke doubled the number of voters by granting the vote to every male householder in the land regardless of what rent he paid.

The opposition, which had done very little more than talk about a reform while in power for the seven preceding years, immediately attacked Disraeli's new bill even though they knew in their hearts that they could not vote against it with a clear conscience. They were still jealous of him. They fought him with every means at their disposal. Gladstone was particularly vehement.

However, Disraeli now knew just how to handle his enemies. He demanded the floor again and again to answer their charges and plead his cause. During the months that the bill was before the House he spoke almost three hundred times. He was now, after long years of experience, a true master of parliamentary action. He knew every device. And so before the bill came to a vote, he was in complete control of both Houses.

Victory was his.

Alone, and almost singlehandedly, Disraeli had not only defeated the strong opposition but also made his party the symbol of reform in England.

When the battle was over he was wildly cheered in the House. He was cheered again in the corridors as he was leaving the building. And stopping in at the Carlton Club on the way home he was cheered once more. In fact, the welcome he received at that Tory stronghold was such as had never before taken place within its walls. The members crowded about him shaking his hand, shouting themselves hoarse and drinking his health.

When the turmoil finally subsided they begged him to stay at the club to dine and celebrate with them but he excused himself. He drove home where his devoted Mary Anne was waiting.

Next day she told a friend, "Dizzy came straight home to me. I had got a pie ready and a bottle of champagne. He ate half the pie and drank all the champagne. And he said to me, 'My dear, you are more to me than a wife.'"

Disraeli, Mary Anne and all his friends were jubilant. But the impact of his victory went even further. The great indefinable public felt that they had found a friend, a champion. And the name Disraeli, or Dizzy, was praised everywhere.

Dizzy's popularity with the people, especially the educated youth of England, had been growing over the years. When he had received an honorary degree at Oxford in 1853, he was given a wildly enthusiastic welcome, a welcome not accorded the other celebrities—Lord Derby, Gladstone, Macaulay and Bulwer Lytton—who were also present. Now going to Scotland to receive another honorary degree from the ancient University of Edinburgh, similar scenes were enacted.

The freedom of the city was conferred upon him. And speaking one evening to a meeting of workingmen, he was cheered over and over again. Referring to this the next day, Disraeli said, "We were so delighted with our reception, Mrs. Disraeli and I, that after we got home we actually danced a jig (or was it a hornpipe?) in our bedroom."

There was still more good fortune awaiting Disraeli. Very shortly after the passage of the Reform Bill, Prime Minister Derby, who was sixty-nine years old, became quite ill. He had been suffering from gout for some time, but now his attacks became more frequent and terribly severe. He sent his resignation to the queen with a recommendation that Disraeli should be appointed in his place.

The queen was extremely pleased. Lord Derby, whom Dizzy had always served with devotion, sent Disraeli heartfelt congratulations, "You have fairly and most honorably won your way to the highest round of the political ladder, and long may you continue to retain your position." Even his enemies bowed in respect saying that his was a "triumph of industry, courage and patience."

At last! At last! Disraeli had realized the ambition of his life. To a friend who offered his congratulations Disraeli said with sarcasm, "Yes, I have climbed to the top of the greasy pole."

When he went down to Parliament for the first time after becoming prime minister, he was loudly cheered in the outer yard, the cheers so loud and sustained that they echoed through the long corridors of that historic building. When he entered the House of Commons, the battleground of his career, the very hall that had reverberated with derisive laughter, hoots and catcalls when he delivered his maiden speech, that same hall now, also, resounded with wild cheers.

To celebrate Dizzy's achievement, Mary Anne gave a great reception. It was attended by everyone of importance, including even Gladstone.

Dizzy was in high spirits as he escorted the Princess of Wales around the rooms. But Mary Anne, on the arm of the Prince of Wales, seemed strangely sad in spite of her smiles and chatter. To some who recorded the event she looked "very ill and haggard."

Many years before when she had caught her finger in the carriage door, she had borne the pain in silence because she did not want to upset Dizzy just before he was to make an important speech. And now once more she was silent, keeping a dark secret locked in her heart, in order to spare him as long as possible from a dreadful sorrow and avoid tarnishing the brilliance of his victory celebration.

It was true, Mary Anne did look "very ill and haggard" for she had only recently learned that she was suffering from cancer of the stomach. However, no one else in the room knew her secret. And so in spite of the weather outside—it was raining in torrents and a high wind was driving the rain with fury—everyone present was happy and gay.

# 13 MRS. DIZZY

◆◆◆◆◆◆◆◆◆◆◆◆◆◆◆◆◆◆◆◆◆◆◆◆◆◆◆◆◆◆◆◆◆◆◆◆◆◆◆◆◆◆◆◆

THE QUEEN ADMIRED DISRAELI'S FRANKNESS, HIS PO-
litical judgment, his vision and his wisdom. She was
deeply impressed by his devotion to England and by his
dream for the future of his country. And she spoke more
frankly to him than she had to any of her previous prime
ministers.

Disraeli, on the other hand, always consulted the
queen, speaking out honestly and openly on all questions.

One of Victoria's ladies-in-waiting described Dizzy
and the queen: "He was never the least shy; he did not
trouble to insinuate; he said what he meant in terms most
surprising, the most unconventional; and the queen
thought she had never in her life seen so amusing a person. He gratified her by his bold assumptions of her

knowledge; she excused his florid adulation on the ground that it was 'oriental,' and she was pleased with the audacious way in which he broke through the ice that surrounded her. He would ask across the dinner table, 'Madam, did Lord Melbourne ever tell your Majesty that you were not to do this or that?' and the queen would take it as the best of jokes."

Disraeli said that he never contradicted the queen. But in matters of importance he always managed to bring her around to his point of view. His powers of persuasion were great.

However, when persuasion failed, he resorted to a more direct method. Very politely he laid down the law as the following message to the queen clearly shows:

Mr. Disraeli wishes not to conceal the infinite pain with which he thus seems to differ on so great a question, from a sovereign to whom he is bound by every tie of personal devotion. . . . His idea of the perfect relation between the sovereign and her minister is that there should be on her part perfect confidence; on his, perfect devotion. In the blended influence of two such sentiments, so ennobling and so refined, he sees the best security for Your Majesty's happiness and the welfare of the realm.

Disraeli could be firm, almost stern with the queen, but his usual manner was light and amusing. Writing to her concerning the new minister of the exchequer whom he had chosen to fill the post he had vacated to become prime minister, he said:

Mr. Disraeli ought to observe to Her Majesty that Mr. Ward Hunt's appearance is rather remarkable but anything but displeasing. He is more than six feet four inches in stature, but doesn't look so tall from his proportionate breadth; like St. Peter's at Rome no one is at first aware of his dimensions. But he has the sagacity of the elephant as well as its form.

No one else would have dared to write the queen such an informal message. But she loved it. Never before had she been treated so humanly. Never before had she been informed on everything that went on behind the scenes in Parliament, at cabinet meetings and during intimate conferences in clubs and private sitting rooms. And she began to form a strong dislike for all those who opposed her Mr. Disraeli.

Yes, Queen Victoria really liked Disraeli. Their natures complimented each other. And her relationship with him grew more personal each day.

One day Mary Anne received a box by royal messenger. It was moss-lined and contained fresh primroses from Windsor and a note written by one of the queen's young daughters, Princess Christian. "Mamma desires me to send you the accompanying flowers in her name for Mr. Disraeli," it said. "She heard him say one day that he was so fond of May and of all those lovely spring flowers that she has ventured to send him these, as they will make his rooms look so bright." After that, every week, primroses from Windsor and violets from Osborne arrived at the Disraeli home in Park Lane.

Disraeli sent the queen copies of all his books. She sent him a copy of her *Leaves from the Journal of Our Life in the Highlands.* He thanked her saying that its pages were filled with "a freshness and fragrance . . . like the heather amid which it was written." When speaking with the queen, he now sometimes said, "We authors, Madam . . ."

Dizzy served as prime minister at this period for only nine months. During this time he passed a Corrupt Practices Bill providing that bribery and other misdemeanors at elections should be dealt with in the courts and not by politicians; he sent troops to Abyssinia to release the British consul who had been imprisoned there during a local war, thus greatly enhancing British prestige in the East; he took over the newly established electric telegraph system for the post office; and he outlawed the gruesome practice of public executions. He was working on a plan for compulsory free education when the end of his service came.

His downfall was brought about by his old enemy Gladstone; Palmerston and Russell were dead. The issue concerned the Anglican Church in Ireland.

Disraeli firmly believed that the State Church, the Anglican Church, was an integral part of the British government. Gladstone contended that in Ireland, where an overwhelming majority of the people were Catholics, the State and the Church should be separate. He said that a Catholic country, ruled by England, should not be required to support a Protestant church.

There was, of course, a great deal of truth in Gladstone's contention. However, his primary reason for making a political issue of this question was to destroy Disraeli, of whom he was intensely jealous and whom he looked upon as the devil himself!

He traveled all through the country on what Disraeli called a "pilgrimage of passion," delivering one speech after another attacking Disraeli's stand. The result was that in December of 1868, following a general election, Disraeli was forced to send in his resignation, and Gladstone became prime minister.

Having fulfilled his childhood dream of being prime minister, Disraeli was now discouraged. Somehow it had all come too late, and it had been so short-lived.

He was sixty-four and Mary Anne seventy-seven years of age. He considered retiring and going to live in the country he loved so passionately, amid the trees and flowers at Hughenden.

But he could not abandon his party in defeat. Besides, the queen had said that the country needed him in Parliament.

To honor retired prime ministers, it was the custom to bestow upon them a title. The queen now suggested that Disraeli accept this honor. It would lighten his burden while still keeping him in the government. With a title he could serve in the House of Lords as an elder statesman.

Disraeli was very pleased but he refused any honor. The House of Lords was not a place of political influence. If he were to remain in politics he wanted to be in the midst of the battle just as he had always been. So he decided to remain as simply Mr. Disraeli and lead the opposition in the Commons.

However, while refusing honors for himself, Disraeli asked the queen to grant him a wish which was very close to his heart. He asked that she elevate Mary Anne, suggesting that her title be Viscountess of Beaconsfield. Beaconsfield was a town close to their beloved Hughenden. Queen Victoria was delighted to do as Disraeli asked.

The queen did not know of Mary Anne's incurable illness. However, Dizzy now knew. Mary Anne had finally told him. And there was nothing he would not do for her, his beloved wife. His letter of gratitude to the queen began with the words, "Mr. Disraeli at your Majesty's feet . . ."

As leader of the opposition, Disraeli naturally attacked Prime Minister Gladstone's Irish Church Bill. His attack was strong but his followers somehow felt that it lacked his usual fire. When he barely voiced any opposition to Gladstone's Education Act, which made elementary education compulsory, they began to question his leadership.

Their doubts became much stronger in 1870 when he suddenly published his first novel in twenty-two years, a romantic satire entitled *Lothair*. They asked each other whether a serious political leader should spend his time with such trivia. Was it becoming to a man who had been prime minister, and who was in direct line to hold that honored office a second time, to publicize his name in such a manner?

When *Lothair* became a best seller—one edition following another in England, eighty thousand copies being sold in the United States in six months—and streets, songs, perfumes and ships were named after its characters, they shook their heads in complete disapproval. A group formed in Parliament whose avowed purpose was to replace Disraeli with the son of Lord Derby, Disraeli's old political friend who had just died.

Disraeli's apparent lack of interest in politics was due to several things: he was very worried about Mary Anne, he was waiting patiently for Gladstone to compound his mistakes and thereby lose his popularity, and he was building up a large party organization which would be ready to strike when Gladstone began to falter.

However, when Disraeli learned of the conspiracy against him, he jumped into action. He immediately offered to resign. And since the prospect of the future without Disraeli was more than any of his colleagues in Parliament could bear, the group was dissolved, apologies were offered, and Disraeli returned to his task as leader of the opposition.

Disraeli had won, but the disloyalty which had been exhibited by his colleagues had shaken his confidence. He wondered if he would ever again be prime minister.

Disraeli had never traveled through the country "stumping" as Gladstone and other political leaders did. He rarely spoke except to his own constituents and in the

House of Commons. But the people everywhere knew of him and trusted him. They recognized that, unlike other politicians, he was a solid, forward-looking individual who had their welfare at heart and whose greatest desire was to better England and the Empire. Now quite miraculously, when unknown to them he needed it most, they demonstrated their trust.

The first indication of this was displayed in the fall of 1871 when the "young politicians" of Scotland made him Lord Rector of Glasgow University. The second sign occurred in February 1872 when the Prince of Wales, followed by all the leading public figures of the day, drove to St. Paul's Cathedral to offer prayers of thanksgiving for the prince's recovery from typhoid fever. The crowds which lined the streets were very cool to Gladstone, but gave Disraeli a rousing ovation. Their cheers greeted him all along the route and back to the very door of his home in Park Lane. Then at Easter when he and Mary Anne went to Manchester, he received still another stirring welcome. The crowds drew their carriage through the streets and deputations paraded in his honor in a pouring rain.

Yes, he now knew that he would again be prime minister.

The trip to Manchester proved too much for Mary Anne. She became very ill, but she rallied and during the next few months was able to attend a few social functions. She said that her strength and spirit were due to Dizzy's constant care and love. And she added, "Thanks to his kindness, my life has been simply one long scene of happiness."

In July it became clear that Mary Anne's condition was critical. She could not eat and had constant pain. Dizzy never left her except to go to the Commons and then he sent her little notes by special messenger. One read, "Dizzy to Mrs. Dizzy, I have nothing to tell you except that I love you. . . ." Her reply was, "Mrs. Dizzy to Dizzy, My own dearest, I miss you sadly. . . . I feel so grateful for your tender love and kindness. . . . Your own devoted Beaconsfield."

Mary Anne was too weak to journey to Hughenden and so they spent the summer in London. Whenever possible Dizzy took her out driving. In October Mary Anne expressed the wish to go to Hughenden. A few weeks later it was obvious that the end was not far off. Disraeli wrote to his faithful secretary, Montagu Corry, "To see her every day weaker and weaker is heart rending. . . . To witness this gradual death . . . unmans me."

At the beginning of December, unable to face it anymore alone, he wired Corry to come. On December 15, 1872, she died.

A letter which she had left to be opened after her death read:

My own dear Husband,
            If I should depart this life before you, leave orders that we may be buried in the same grave at whatever distance you may die from England.

And now God bless you, my kindest, dearest! You have been a perfect husband to me. Be put by my side in the same grave. And now, farewell, my dear Dizzy. Do not live alone, dearest. Some one I earnestly hope you may find as attached to you as your own devoted

Mary Anne.

She was buried in the churchyard at Hughenden.

Queen Victoria, the Prince and Princess of Wales, foreign monarchs, ambassadors, lord and ladies, members of Parliament, the neighborhood farmers and other simple people all over England sent heartfelt messages of sympathy. Gladstone forgot his envy of Disraeli for a moment and wrote him a kindly letter.

Dizzy said, "There was no care that she could not mitigate, and no difficulty which she could not face. She was the most cheerful and courageous woman I ever knew."

Even though Disraeli had been expecting Mary Anne's death for a long time and even though he was grateful that her agony was over, he was completely crushed. They had been married for thirty-three years. He was now sixty-eight years old.

Mary Anne's money and the house in Park Lane, where she and Dizzy had lived for so long, belonged to the estate of her first husband, Wyndham Lewis. While Mary Anne had had the use of both during her lifetime, they now reverted to his heirs. And so Dizzy was forced to move to a hotel.

To leave the home where he and she had been so happy was like a second parting. This was the house where Mary Anne had waited for him night after night when he had been forced to stay late at Parliament. He had been able to see the glow of its brightly lighted windows from afar as his carriage made its way through the cold foggy night. Here was the home where he had always found the comfort of understanding and love. Now it was taken from him, and the prospect of spending the rest of his life alone in a small apartment in some impersonal hotel frightened him. He said rather pathetically, "I hope some of my friends will take notice of me now in my misfortune, for I have no home. And when I tell my coachman to drive *home* I feel it is a mockery."

But he need not have worried, for his friends understood his sudden loneliness and did everything possible to make this sad time easier for him. Corry watched over him like a son. Quiet supper parties were arranged by others. And he was often in the homes of Baron Rothschild and Lord John Manners, one of the original three young men who had founded "Young England."

In July 1873, Disraeli returned to Hughenden, where he began sorting out a whole roomful of papers that Mary Anne had collected. He found every letter he had ever written to her, even the brief notes addressed, "Dizzy to Mrs. Dizzy."

He also found hundreds of letters from old friends, many of whom were now long dead. This collection, formed a firsthand record of the time, a record which historians have found invaluable.

Mary Anne had been unable to part with anything that was related to him. When she cut his hair, as she did every second week of their married life, she saved the cuttings in little envelopes. There were over one thousand of these!

Toward the end of August, Disraeli told Corry that the task was finished. "She died for me one hundred times in the heart-rending, but absolutely inevitable, process," he said.

# 14 INDIA AND SUEZ

✦✦✦✦✦✦✦✦✦✦✦✦✦✦✦✦✦✦✦✦✦✦✦✦✦✦✦✦✦✦✦✦✦✦✦✦✦✦✦✦

MANY OF DISRAELI'S FRIENDS FEARED THAT THE LOSS of Mary Anne would force Disraeli into retirement. But the air was charged with political excitement. This to Dizzy was the wine of life. And so to escape his mournful recollections, he plunged into the battle.

The political pendulum was swinging back into Disraeli's favor. Gladstone was rapidly losing his popularity. Realizing this, Gladstone offered to resign, but when the queen invited Disraeli to form a new government he refused. He said that his majority was too small. He wanted to come to office with a large majority so that he could not be overthrown for several years.

Gladstone, being a very sharp politician, tried to force Disraeli to accept the office of prime minister. But Disraeli would not allow himself to be maneuvered into an awkward position. He was too keen for Gladstone. And so after several days of arguing back and forth, Gladstone was forced to continue in office.

Having settled this problem, Disraeli sat back and waited. He would give Gladstone plenty of opportunity to compound his blunders. Then, when the public had had its fill, it would decide who would become prime minister.

And this is just what happened. When a general election was finally called in February 1874, Disraeli's Conservative party won a sweeping victory. He had a clear majority of fifty seats over all the other parties combined, and one hundred seats more than Gladstone's Liberal party.

Queen Victoria was overjoyed. She had never liked Gladstone, who was so austere and, also, hysterical that she questioned his sanity. And she quickly approved of his resignation and sent for Disraeli.

Disraeli lost no time forming an able cabinet and setting out to prove the principle, established by the American Revolution, that governments exist solely for the benefit of the governed. He was determined to establish his party as the party of democracy. During the six years which followed, while he served as prime minister, great social reforms took place.

His government passed laws to shorten work hours in factories, give workmen legal equality with their employers, guarantee the people's savings, clear slum areas, improve sanitation and end the pollution of rivers. His government also passed a law to protect seamen, the Plimsoll Act, which in one form or another was later adopted by so many other countries that its principle has become international.

An alarming number of British sailors were lost at sea each year due to the greed of shipowners. Many ships were not seaworthy and all were overloaded. Riding low in the waters they were easy prey to high seas. The shipowners did not care because their ships and cargoes were insured. As for the sailors who drowned, they did not matter! Merchandise was valuable. Life was cheap!

Plimsoll, a member of Commons, proposed a bill requiring that a line be painted on all vessels showing the depth to which they might safely be submerged through loading. It was a just bill, but at first was voted down in the Commons because the powerful shipping interests and merchants controlled a lot of votes. Plimsoll was so angry that he lost his temper and, shaking both fists in the air, cried out against the offending members, "Scoundrels! Scoundrels!"

Disraeli was forced to reprimand Plimsoll for his outburst, but recommended that the bill be brought up a second time. This time many of the men who had voted against the first bill were ashamed, and so the Plimsoll measure became law. The "Plimsoll Line" became mandatory on every British ship, as it is to this day.

Two other matters which occupied Disraeli on the home front were the church and artists and scientists.

Under the direction of the archbishop of Canterbury and the queen he brought about certain reforms within the church and extended its influence by creating six new dioceses. And having always placed a high value upon men of letters, he said that it was regrettable that England did not have the equivalent of the Legion of Honor. Lacking this he suggested to the queen that the famous physicist George Stokes receive a knighthood and that the poet Alfred Tennyson be made a baronet. He also felt that the historian and essayist Thomas Carlyle, who had spent his life in poverty, should be offered the Grand Cross of the Order of the Bath, plus a pension.

Queen Victoria agreed and Disraeli wrote to all three men. But both Tennyson and Carlyle declined any honors. Tennyson asked that after his death the baronetcy be conferred on his son instead. And Carlyle wrote, "Titles of honor, of all degrees, are out of keeping with the tenor of my poor life." Concerning a pension he said, ". . . after years of rigorous and frugal, but, thank God, never degrading poverty, money has become amply abundant even superabundant. . . ." And he ended his letter with these words of praise—he said that Disraeli's offer was, "magnanimous and noble, without example in the history of governing persons with men of letters."

Disraeli was deeply interested in affairs at home, but he was equally interested in the future of the British Empire.

While Gladstone had been prime minister, Disraeli had kept a close watch on foreign affairs, and what he had seen had not pleased him. Russia had been adding one area after another to her already vast land. Having made political inroads into Afghanistan, she was now a threat to India. Bismarck, whom Disraeli called "another old Bonaparte," had consolidated the many independent German principalities into one strong and aggressive nation. Just four years before, in 1870, he had hurled this powerful force against France. He was now seeking a pretext to launch a second onslaught on France, and he had his eye on Belgium.

Gladstone, who was only interested in home affairs, had ignored all this, and Russia and Germany had naturally concluded that England was weak and disinterested and could be ignored. Disraeli was determined to correct this misconception.

Learning that the czar of Russia and the emperor of Germany were to hold a meeting, Dizzy informed the Russian ambassador in London that England would support a move for peace in Europe by the czar. He also got the queen to write personal notes to both of these powerful rulers.

The united strength of England and Russia could not be ignored, and Bismarck was forced to abandon his plan for attacking Beligum and France. He was checked. Disraeli, not wasting one precious moment, immediately ordered a substantial increase in the British army and navy.

Disraeli now turned his attention to India, on which Russia was casting covetous glances.

Numerous rivalries and differences divided the princes

and peoples of the various states which made up that vast land. This created a weakness of which Russia could take advantage; she could pick off one small kingdom at a time, so Disraeli was anxious to unite the Indian states into one strong nation.

He felt that the best way to bring about this unity was to give all the different peoples of India a common interest, namely, to strengthen their ties to the English throne. And so he arranged for the Prince of Wales to go on a tour of India.

During the prince's visit Dizzy appointed a new viceroy of India. He was Lord Lytton, the son of his old friend, the novelist Bulwer Lytton. Disraeli had known this young lord since he was a small boy and he trusted him. He knew that Lord Lytton would fit in with his plans. First of all, he would take care of the Prince of Wales and see that he met all the richest and most powerful princes of India, cementing their bonds to England. Then later, he would arrange for the final and as yet secret part of Disraeli's plan for uniting India and strengthening her ties to the throne. Young Lord Lytton, he felt, was just the right person to help him in having Victoria crowned empress of India!

The Prince of Wales' tour was a tremendous success. The Indian princes were delighted to have in their midst this royal visitor, the eldest son of Queen Victoria and heir-apparent. They treated him with every grace and sent the queen fabulous jewels in homage.

When news of its success reached England, Disraeli

thought the time had come to crown Victoria empress. He made his plan known. Victoria was, of course, overjoyed but there were many in England who objected. Some said that the title of empress was not in English tradition and others argued that the empresses had often been women of low morals. Gladstone went into "white rages." But Dizzy was not to be put off, and he went ahead oiling the complicated machinery of government.

In 1876, he persuaded Queen Victoria to open Parliament in person, an official act which she had seldom undertaken since the death of Prince Albert fifteen years before. Her presence created such excitement among the members that Disraeli was almost knocked down in the rush. But he did not mind because he felt their enthusiasm would help him achieve his aim. He was right. The necessary approval was won, and finally on January 1, 1877, Viceroy Lord Lytton, before a great gathering of princes in Delhi, proclaimed Queen Victoria empress of India.

On that same evening, while the Indian princes gathered in Delhi were saluting Victoria as "Monarch of Monarchs," Disraeli dined with the queen and her court at Windsor. To his surprise he found that she had set aside her usual simple black dress and had adorned herself with masses of jewels which she had received from the Indian princes.

At dinner, breaking all court etiquette, Disraeli rose to propose the health of the queen of England and "empress of India" and to make a speech in her honor which one of the court ladies described as being "as flowery as the oration of a maharajah."

When Disraeli had concluded, the queen's court was amazed for a second time. The queen rose and, smiling with the greatest of pleasure, bowed and curtsied slightly to Mr. Disraeli.

By checking Germany in Europe and Russia in the East and by proclaiming Victoria empress of India, Disraeli had elevated the British Empire to an eminence which it had never held before. But as though this were not enough, during this same time, Disraeli had accomplished one more brilliant feat: he had secured a new trade route between England and the East.

One day, November 15, 1875, Dizzy accidentally heard that Ismail Pasha, the khedive, or viceroy, of Egypt, was in great need of money and was trying to sell his shares in the Suez Canal to a French syndicate. Dizzy immediately hooked upon the idea of buying this controlling interest for England. The Suez Canal was the gateway to India. But Lord Derby, head of the foreign office, was not very keen about the idea, saying that the Suez Canal was too far away.

Undaunted, Disraeli reviewed the history of the canal and began to formulate a plan of action. About twenty-five years before, a French engineer named de Lesseps had obtained a concession from Said Pasha, who was then khedive of Egypt, to build a canal linking the Mediterranean with the Red Sea. In return for this right, Said

Pasha had received almost half of the shares in the Suez Canal Company. The remaining shares had been sold to the French public to raise money for the construction. England had been asked to participate but she had refused on the ridiculous ground that the canal would harm her shipping, a very shortsighted view shared by several former prime ministers.

When the canal was finally opened, in 1869, England found that instead of being harmful to her shipping, the canal was very beneficial. It reduced the route to India and the Far East by many days. In the six years which had passed since then many hundreds of ships of all nations had gone through its locks each year, paying a heavy toll for the privilege. Half of these ships were British. And Disraeli foresaw that very soon, with the constantly increasing growth of trade between England and the Orient, three-quarters of all the ships using the canal would be British.

All this Dizzy knew; this and more. "What would happen in case of war?" he asked. "Would British warships be allowed to use the canal?"

The more Disraeli turned the Suez Canal problem over in his mind, the more it grew in importance. Losing no further time he wired a British representative in Egypt to get all necessary information. A return wire confirmed the fact that the khedive was eager to sell his shares for immediate cash. He had already given an option, which would expire on the following Tuesday, to a French company. Would the khedive do business with England? The khedive said, "Yes." He did not care where the money came from, for he was on the verge of bankruptcy. The amount? Four million pounds, a sum equal to twenty million dollars.

This information, which Dizzy got quickly over long-distance telegraph from Egypt on November 18, he transmitted to the queen. She at once saw the importance of having an interest in the canal and gave her approval.

"Scarcely breathing time," said Dizzy. "But the thing must be done."

Dizzy now wired the English ambassador in Paris, who went to the French foreign minister and told him very frankly that since most of the ships using the canal were British, England did not like to see the Egyptian shares going to a second French company.

The French government was exceedingly grateful to Disraeli and Queen Victoria for the firm stand they had taken against Bismarck earlier that very year, saving France from a second brutal German invasion. So France was glad to do as England asked. The Paris banks were informed that the French government did not approve of a second French company investing in the Suez Canal. Without the banks the money could not be raised. And so on the appointed Tuesday, the French option lapsed. On November 25, just ten days after Disraeli first started acting in this very complicated matter, a paper was signed in Cairo by which England contracted to buy the khedive's shares in the Suez Canal.

But two important things were still missing—permission and money. And Dizzy had to get both within a few hours.

Disraeli needed Parliament's consent and Parliament was not in session. To put the deal through without Parliament, Dizzy had to have the unanimous consent of his cabinet, and two of his ministers needed to be convinced.

There was also a problem about the money. Dizzy knew that if he applied to the Bank of England for such a large sum it would require a meeting of the directors and would take many days. There was also the great danger of the news leaking out; a deal involving four million pounds could create a serious disturbance, even a panic, in the stock market. The Bank of England was out. He would have to find the money elsewhere.

He lost no time and quickly called a meeting of his ministers, instructing Corry to wait in the anteroom, hat in hand, ready to receive his signal. The signal was very simple, just one word, "Yes." From there on Corry knew just what he had to do.

Dizzy was confident that he would win over his two balking ministers. And he did, with arguments built on reason. He spoke of the future of the Empire, of trade and of the fact that Gladstone had so neglected foreign affairs that in case of war, England would find herself in a most difficult situation.

Since time was of the essence, he talked quickly. And he gained the needed consent.

When Corry got the "Yes" signal he rushed straight to Baron Rothschild, whom he found seated at the dinner table. He told Rothschild that the prime minister needed four million pounds for a very special purpose and that he needed it on the following day.

The baron listened but did not reply, concentrating all his attention on some grapes he was eating. Then turning to Disraeli's young secretary, he asked, "What is your security?"

"The British government," Corry replied.

"Tell the prime minister he shall have it."

Corry rushed back to Downing Street where Dizzy was waiting.

Disraeli sat down at his desk and quickly wrote a note to the queen. "It is just settled. You have it, Madam . . . Four millions sterling! and almost immediately. There was only one firm that could do it—Rothschild's. They behaved admirably; advanced the money at a low rate and the entire interest of the khedive is now yours, Madam."

Dizzy was proud of his Suez accomplishment. He loved nothing better than playing for high stakes. And he said without modesty but with complete truth, "Alone I did it."

The queen was also delighted. The Prince of Wales, returning from India saw with pride the Union Jack flying at Suez. Everyone in England approved and was overjoyed, except, of course, Gladstone, who would not admit the importance of Suez and who raved against Disraeli calling him a "villain" and "an agent of Satan."

Many of the kings of Europe sent their congratulations to the queen. The czar, however, was silent. Suez was very close to Turkey, and Turkey had something that Russia badly needed—the Dardanelles, the gateway to the Black Sea and her southern ports. Having no port in Europe except in the cold, winter-locked Baltic, Russia was also planning to drive the heathen Turk out of Europe and secure ports on the Mediterranean.

Bismarck was another who sent no congratulations to the queen. He had risen to power because Gladstone, while prime minister, had been indifferent to affairs abroad. But now England was fast growing into a first-class world power and Disraeli was the man responsible for her rise.

# 15 THE EARL OF BEACONSFIELD

◆◇◆◇◆◇◆◇◆◇◆◇◆◇◆◇◆◇◆◇◆◇◆◇◆◇◆◇◆◇◆◇◆◇◆◇◆

ONLY A FEW MONTHS AFTER TAKING OFFICE, DISRAELI suffered a severe attack of gout. He was in terrible pain and could not attend the Commons. The queen was very worried. She advised him not to sit in overheated rooms because the sudden change in temperature when he went out would be most harmful.

Eventually he felt better and returned to his full schedule of work, but the queen's concern for him did not diminish. One day when he went to the palace to report to her, she said, "To think of you having the gout all the time! . . . And you ought not to stand now. You shall have a chair!"

Dizzy was deeply touched by her consideration but he refused. Court etiquette did not allow him to sit in her

165

presence during an audience. But the queen was insistent and he capitulated. However, he was ever careful to erase the evidence, always replacing the chair to its proper place in the room before leaving.

Disraeli's gout had become bearable, but the heavy duties of his office now began to attack his frail and aging body. He developed asthma. Every speech exhausted him; his life was endangered. Still he carried on. He said, "One must take risks in life, or else it would be as dull as death."

Less than a year after England's sensational purchase of an interest in the Suez Canal, trouble broke out between Russia and Turkey. Russia had been infiltrating Turkish possessions in the Balkans, with secret societies and special agents. In an attempt to wipe out these subversive groups, the Turks had engaged in a series of unspeakable massacres. All Europe was revolted at the cruelty and ruthlessness of the "heathen" Turk. Many in England, even members of Parliament, said that the Turks should be driven out of Europe and confined to the Orient. Gladstone was one who voiced this opinion—very loudly.

Dizzy, however, held a different view. He considered Russia as a much greater danger to Europe than the disorganized and corrupt Turkish Empire. With keen insight into Russia's intentions, he warned that the czar would like to build a second Kremlin on the Bosporus and that if the Turks were driven out of Europe, the Russians would quickly occupy all the eastern shores of

the Mediterranean Sea. This would present a serious
threat to England's lifeline to the East, especially to India. That land might be the next to fall prey. He said,
"I am as anxious as anyone to keep well with the Russians, but there is no acting with people when you cannot
feel sure they are telling the truth."

Dizzy's position was awkward indeed. He had to find a
way of defending Turkey against all public sentiment,
sentiment which was being whipped up into a white fury
by Gladstone. He spoke in the House time after time,
appealing to reason. In private he called Gladstone's behavior "treasonable" and said that the man himself was
a maniac, envious and hypocritical and "whether preach-
ing, praying, speechifying, or scribbling—never a gentleman!"

Then one tiring day, he concluded a moving speech
in the House with these words, "What our duty is at this
critical moment is to maintain the Empire of England."

Having finished his speech Disraeli looked wistfully at
the benches and at the speaker's chair. There were tears
in his eyes. Then taking the arm of his faithful Corry he
walked out slowly, as though he were walking in his own
funeral.

His colleagues looked on in wonder. What was the
meaning of it all? They did not know that the words they
had just heard were the last words Disraeli would ever
speak in that great hall of Commons, the hall which had
been the site of so many of his victories, the hall which
for thirty-nine years had reverberated with his marvelous

voice. Only the next morning did they learn that he would no longer be with them. His health had gone from bad to worse, and he had finally consented to allow the queen to bestow upon him the title of Earl of Beaconsfield and Viscount Hughenden. He would, henceforth, sit in the House of Lords.

Disraeli's colleagues were moved. They knew that his age—he was now seventy-two years old—and his poor health had forced this move. One said, "All the real chivalry and delight of party politics seem to have departed. Nothing remains but routine." Another said, "The days of the giants are over."

It was only natural that they should feel this way, but Disraeli had not retired. He fully intended to keep on fighting.

When the queen opened the next session of Parliament, Lord Beaconsfield stood at her side dressed in scarlet and ermine. In his hands he held aloft the great Sword of State. Now all could see that Dizzy was still the defender of England.

In April 1877, the czar, encouraged by Gladstone's reckless speeches into believing that England was with him, finally declared war against Turkey. And Disraeli, suffering from another attack of gout, was flat on his back in bed.

Gladstone used this opportunity to intensify his hysterical campaign against the "heathens" with more "atrocity agitation" and with demands for war against

Turkey. To complicate matters still further, Queen Victoria, who dreaded the Russians and was irritated that no action had been taken to stop them, became petulant. She wrote Disraeli that "if England is to kiss Russia's feet, I will lay down my crown."

Then there were the doctors. One advised Disraeli to go to Bournemouth for a rest; another said he should go to Ems. Disraeli had a different idea. He said, "I should like to send them both to Jericho."

It was a very trying time for him, but since there was no one in England who could fight more courageously when there was fighting to be done, he rose to the task. He sent a message of warning to the czar, stating that England would not remain neutral unless Russia respected three points important to the British Empire: the Suez Canal, the Dardanelles and Constantinople.

While replying that the question of Constantinople could be settled by a congress of European powers, the czar gave orders to his chief of staff to capture that great city. He felt that occupation was the first step toward possession.

The queen was alarmed at this news and tried to get Disraeli to send troops. She was anxious that war be declared on Russia. Disraeli was anxious to avoid war. He said, "Oh, if the queen were a man, she would go and give those Russians . . . such a beating!"

The situation went from bad to worse with each passing hour. England ordered her fleet to proceed to Constantinople. It looked as though war were inevitable. The armed forces were increased and the London docks were piled high with war material. Then suddenly came the good news that Russia and Turkey were engaged in peace talks.

The British fleet was recalled at once. Disraeli waited hopefully. However, when he learned of the terms he felt that Russia's demands on Turkey were excessive. While Russia respected his wishes on the Suez, she was demanding complete domination of the Balkans and part of Armenia and control of the Dardanelles, a fact which was of great importance to the British Empire.

Disraeli now acted decisively. "If we are bold and determined we shall secure peace," he said, "and dictate its conditions to Europe. . . . We have to maintain the Empire. . . ." He told Russia either to withdraw from Constantinople or allow the Dardanelles to be occupied by Britain or a neutral power. And he demanded that all Russian peace terms with Turkey be submitted to an international congress for acceptance or rejection.

Russia naturally ignored Disraeli's demands, but England's prime minister was not to be put off. He ordered the fleet to proceed at once to Constantinople and he secretly brought seven thousand Indian troops into the Mediterranean and, in a surprise attack, took the Island of Malta.

Russia, who did not want war with England, now bowed to Disraeli's will. She agreed to submit all her demands on Turkey to a congress.

This at once brought the arrogant Bismarck into the

act. He pretended to be perfectly neutral, which he was not, and insisted that Germany act as mediator and host. And he got his way. It was decided that the peace congress would be held in Berlin.

Disraeli naturally wanted to represent England at the congress, but the queen disapproved. She was very worried about his health. He had recently had an attack of asthma so severe that he had been forced to sit up all night, periodically leaning over the back of a chair in order to catch his breath. But the Prince of Wales said, "He is the only man who can show Russia and the other powers that Britain is really in earnest."

Queen Victoria finally consented, and together with Lord Salisbury, the foreign secretary, and his faithful and indispensible Corry, Disraeli set out happily for Berlin. He took the journey in easy stages in order not to tax his health, stopping to visit the king and queen of the Belgians on the way. Arriving in Berlin four days after leaving London, he immediately received a request from Bismarck for a personal meeting.

The English ambassador to Germany told Disraeli that Bismarck wanted to find out exactly how firm his intentions were. Always a political genius, Disraeli decided on a unique device for demonstrating this point. After cordially greeting Bismarck, a grotesque giant of a man with an enormous stomach, red face, yet a strangely gentle voice, he began relating the story of his life. He talked without stopping, inserting many interesting and amusing touches. He began with his childhood and told in detail how he had overcome one obstacle after the other in his fight to reach the top. It was a master stroke for it accomplished two things simultaneously: it established an intimacy between him and Bismarck and at the same time showed Bismarck that he, Disraeli, had never accepted defeat!

Bismarck now realized that Disraeli would impose his will on the congress. Believing as he did in "blood and iron," Bismarck was much impressed by anyone who was willing to fight for what he wanted. He looked upon Disraeli as the outstanding figure at the congress, and went about everywhere saying, "The old Jew, that is the man."

The purpose of the congress was that all nations present might enter into free discussions about the Russian-Turkish treaty. But since diplomacy is always riddled with intrigue, nothing was open and above board. Before the congress opened, each nation had made some secret arrangement with another nation. England had entered into a secret defensive alliance with Turkey, who gave her the Island of Cyprus at the far eastern end of the Mediterranean in order to stop further Russian aggression in that area. This meant that England, which already had Gibraltar and Malta, now controlled the entire Mediterranean Sea. France had secret agreements with Egypt and Syria. Austria had special interests in the Balkans which England and Germany had approved.

Everything was beclouded by intrigue. Two things only were clear. Russia wanted access to the Mediterranean, and since she had won her war of aggression against Turkey, she wanted the spoils.

Disraeli was like a rock. He could not be moved. He was determined that Russia should not come into the Mediterranean. Despite his arguments and oratory the Russians refused to give an inch. And so after several weeks, Dizzy decided to play a very dangerous card. He decided to use confidence to create rumor, and rumor to set off a war of nerves.

At a dinner party he found himself sitting next to the Italian representative. He knew that this man was one of Bismarck's favorites and that since he represented the most neutral nation in the congress, he had everybody's ear. "I told him in confidence," Disraeli recorded, "and as an old friend that . . . if Russia would not accept our proposals, I had resolved to break up the Congress." And the very next day he instructed Corry to order a special train to carry the entire British delegation back to Calais. The train was to stand ready at the Berlin station.

Disraeli was playing for high stakes, higher than any he had ever played for before. If he failed it would mean war between Russia and England. But he was confident of success, and he sat back calmly waiting for his magic to begin working. As he expected, he did not have to wait long.

Within a few hours the "confidence" he had dropped in the Italian representative's ear had spread throughout the congress, and Bismarck came hurriedly to his hotel.

The Chancellor wanted to know if a compromise was possible. Disraeli said no.

"Am I to understand that this is an ultimatum?"

"You are."

That evening Disraeli and Bismarck met again. Disraeli recorded that this time Bismarck "was convinced that the ultimatum was not a sham, and before I went to bed . . . St. Petersburg had surrendered."

Arriving back in London, Disraeli received a tumultuous welcome. The crowds went wild. Trafalgar Square was a sea of faces and waving hats and handkerchiefs. Downing Street was decorated with red bunting. As he entered the hall of No. 10, he was presented with a huge bouquet of flowers sent by the queen.

The crowds would not disperse. They kept cheering and cheering. At length Dizzy appeared at a window together with Lord Salisbury. He held up his hand for silence. Then he spoke, "We have brought you back, I think, peace with honor."

# 16 "KINGS LOVE HIM THAT SPEAKETH RIGHT."

◇◇◇◇◇◇◇◇◇◇◇◇◇◇◇◇◇◇◇◇◇◇◇◇◇◇◇◇◇◇◇◇◇◇◇◇

QUEEN VICTORIA WAS EXTREMELY PLEASED WITH Disraeli's victory at Berlin. She wanted to make him a marquis or duke but he refused both of these honors. He accepted instead the Order of the Garter and, with his characteristic generosity, asked the queen to bestow the Garter also upon Lord Salisbury whose help had been invaluable to him.

England was very pleased with the results of the congress in Berlin. Germany was pleased. Turkey was pleased. Only Russia was dissatisfied. Having been checked in her aggression in Europe, she now cast her greedy eyes on Afghanistan, whose mountain passes lead directly into India.

Because of this, England was forced to use military

action to rearrange the border between India and Afghanistan in such a way that it would be easy to defend it against Russian advances. The Afghans naturally resented England's attack and Disraeli's government was subjected to much criticism at home.

On top of this came trouble with the Zulus in South Africa. The British commander ignored Disraeli's advice and attacked the Zulus, who were, of course, soon vanquished. But while England was the victor, this affair caused Disraeli much political discomfort and embarrassment.

The criticism leveled at Disraeli's government because of the troubles in Afghanistan and South Africa were increased by troubles at home over which he had no control. A series of five bad harvests and a slump in trade created a recession and unemployment.

Gladstone, of course, took advantage of the moment, traveling through England on another of his "pilgrimages of passion." And since in politics the road is ever rocky and upsets are common, the Liberal party now came back into power with Gladstone once more the prime minister.

Disraeli had now been prime minister for four full years, and during this period his relationship with the queen had grown closer each day. She loved him dearly, and, as far as court etiquette allowed, he expressed the same feelings for her.

He was a frequent guest at Balmoral and the other royal residences. The queen's private yacht was at his disposal to bring him to Osborne on the Isle of Wight whenever he wished. She had even granted him permission to bring Corry along.

The moss-lined boxes of primroses from Windsor and violets from Osborne still arrived every week. She sent him letters almost every day and many presents. She had a painting of herself made expressly for him and asked that he have a portrait painted for her, a request which he immediately fulfilled. People remarked that when she was with him, she smiled all the time. She was actually vivacious, a marked contrast to her usually somber behavior.

He had helped free her of the heavy sorrow which had lain upon her heart ever since Prince Albert died. He brought her out of her deep mourning and popularized her with her people. He admired her intellect. He consulted her on all matters, saying that she knew more about state affairs than anyone else in the country.

His letters to her were filled with warmth. He wrote, "If your Majesty is ill, he [Disraeli] is sure he will himself break down." And, "He lives only for Her, and works only for Her, and without Her he is lost." Following a rare disagreement with her, he wrote to one of her friends, saying, "I love the Queen—perhaps the only person in this world left to me that I love; and therefore you can understand how much it worries and disquiets me when there is a cloud between us." Acknowledging some camellias she had sent him, he wrote, "They are 'more precious than rubies' coming, as they do . . . from a Sovereign whom he adores."

177

When he was ill she was distracted. She sent her personal physician to care for him. Once she came to see him. He wrote to a friend that he had received the queen of England "in slippers and a dressing gown." On another occasion, she went to Hughenden for luncheon, something which was almost unheard of. And on still another occasion, when he came to the palace after a long absence due to illness, she was so delighted that he thought she was going to embrace him.

Queen Victoria was desolate at losing her beloved prime minister, "the kindest and most devoted as well as one of the wisest ministers" she had ever had. In appreciation of his great services, she offered to bestow a title on his nephew, an honor which he declined asking that she elevate instead his secretary, Montagu Corry.

Corry had just inherited Rowton Castle, seven thousand acres of land and an income equivalent to fifty thousand dollars a year. And so the queen took the name of his castle and gave him the title of Lord Rowton.

Because of strict custom, she could see Disraeli only rarely; she saw him, in fact, just three times more during the year which he still had to live.

Disraeli was also deeply distressed by their separation. He said that his visits with the queen had been "almost his only happiness and interest in this world." However, their warm friendship continued as before. Her flowers still arrived to "brighten his rooms," and they wrote each other as often as they had in the past, letters filled with affection. He advised her on all kinds of matters personal and official. She advised him about his health and told him that his portrait on the wall brought her happiness and comfort.

Her letters were usually pleasant and gay. But in one she expressed the deep loneliness she felt. She said that she longed for his strong arm to lean upon. And she concluded with these heart-rending words, "I have no one."

Altogether Disraeli had served as prime minister for six years and the strain had undermined his health. He retired to Hughenden hoping to regain his strength in the peace and quiet of his trees, gardens and park lands. But when the weather was bad his asthma caused him great discomfort. And since the weather was often bad for whole weeks at a time, he suffered almost continually.

However, in spite of this he remained in Hughenden, where he was surrounded by his books. He truly considered them as friends, and what could be better than a house full of friends? Besides, he had something he wanted to do.

One day he placed several quires of large paper upon his desk and began writing a novel. Because of his illness he could do only a little at a sitting, but very soon the pages began to pile up. The story, which he called *Endymion,* was about an ambitious young man who chose politics as his life work and finally rose to the coveted post of prime minister. It was a story he knew well. Once more he had returned to writing about himself and revealing his secret thoughts.

179

Corry persuaded a publisher to advance Disraeli a sum equal to fifty thousand dollars for this new novel, the largest sum advanced for a literary work up to that time. With this money he rented a house on Curzon Street in fashionable Mayfair. The lease was for nine years.

"It will see me out," he said. "I always intended to die in London."

Disraeli spent Christmas at Hughenden and moved into London shortly after the first of the year 1881. He was now seventy-seven years old and his health was failing fast. He had lost a lot of weight. He was stooped. One eye was closed; he could only see out of it by holding the lid open with his fingers. Between his brown wrinkled skin and emaciated body he looked like a walking mummy.

He occasionally strolled around the neighborhood leaning on Corry's arm, dressed in a topcoat lined with black astrakhan. At other times he rode in his carriage to the House of Lords. Sometimes he went out to a dinner party, but these occasions were very rare.

Still he remained interested in everything about him—literature as well as politics. He was always eager to talk to the younger men who were in the House of Commons. "A party is lost," he once said, "if it has not constant reinforcement of young and energetic men."

January, 1881, was icy and cold. During February and the beginning of March there were a few nice days. But at the end of March he caught a chill which brought him to bed.

He felt that the end was approaching. He said, "I shall never survive this attack." Later, he added, "I should prefer to live, but I am not afraid of dying."

His strength was fast running out. The queen was distraught. Her letters and telegrams arrived daily. She suggested a medical consultation. Her wishes were carried out, but nothing could be done to relieve his heavy cough and his violent attacks of asthma.

His room, as always, was filled with violets and primroses from the queen. She was eager to visit him but felt that it would be better if he remained completely "quiet." She wrote him, "You are constantly in my thoughts. . . ."

The end came on April 19, 1881, at two o'clock in the morning. The doctor was present. Corry held his right hand. For a moment it seemed as though the dying man wanted to sit up in bed. He managed to lift himself part way and his lips moved. He was trying to say something. Then he fell back and his eyes closed in a sleep that never wakened. *End*

The British government offered a funeral and tomb in Westminster Abbey, but Disraeli's friends felt that he would have preferred to be buried at Hughenden in the graveyard beside his devoted Mary Anne. And so this was done.

The Prince of Wales attended the funeral and brought two wreaths from the queen. On one was a note which said, "A token of true affection, friendship and respect."

On the other, a wreath of primroses, was a line in the queen's hand. It read, "His favorite flower."

The queen ordered that a tablet be put up in the little church at Hughenden at her expense. The inscription reads: "To the dear and Honoured Memory of Benjamin Earl of Beaconsfield this Memorial is Placed by His Grateful Sovereign and Friend Victoria R. I." The bottom line contains a quotation from Proverbs, "Kings love him that speaketh right."

A few days after the funeral, when peace and quiet had come once more to Hughenden, a woman, alone, came to the little churchyard to visit Disraeli's grave. The vault was opened for her. She placed some flowers upon the coffin. It was Victoria, queen of England and empress of India.

# Bibliography

The great biography of Disraeli in six volumes was begun by William F. Monypenny and finished by George E. Buckle. The first volumes appeared in 1910 and the last in 1920. The Monypenny-Buckle *Life* is the main source for all our modern biographies of Disraeli. This text, which was revised in 1929, presents one of the most complete biographies ever written.

Bolitho, Hector. *The Reign of Queen Victoria.* New York: Macmillan, 1948.

Froude, J. A. *Lord Beaconsfield.* New York: Harper & Bros., 1890.

Fulford, Roger. *Queen Victoria.* London: Collins, 1951.

Harper, Charles G. *A Literary Man's London.* London: Palmer, 1926.

Kebbel, T. E. *Lord Beaconsfield and Other Tory Memories.* Kennerly, 1907.

Maurois, André. *Disraeli.* New York: Appleton, 1928.

Meynell, Wilfrid. *Benjamin Disraeli.* New York: Appleton, 1903.

Pearson, Hasketh. *Dizzy.* New York: Harper & Bros., 1951.

# Index

◆◆◆◆◆◆◆◆◆◆◆◆◆◆◆◆◆◆◆◆◆◆◆◆◆◆◆◆◆◆◆◆◆◆◆◆◆◆◆◆◆◆◆◆

185

his second novel, 45; grieves over death of dearest friend, 50-51; is defeated in run for Parliament, 54-55, 58, 60, 62; writes two more novels, 55-56; becomes literary and social success, 56-57; wants to be prime minister, 58; description of, 59; is given nickname, 60; his friendship with the Lewises, 60, 64; his political philosophy, 61; joins Tory party; 62; is elected, 64; his views, 66; has heavy personal debts, 67-68; his maiden speech, 68-69; attends Victoria's coronation, 71; his feelings for Mary Anne, 72-75; his speeches listened to with interest and respect, 75-76; marriage, 77; speaks for lower classes, 85-86; is leader of Young England group, 89-90; breech widens between him and Peel, 90-91; his new novel published in America, 91; is considered greatest speaker of England, 91-92; helps put through reform bills, 93; favors relief for Ireland, 94-95; writes literature's first labor novel, 97-99; against repeal of Corn Laws, 100-01; his beliefs, 103-04; buys estate, 104-05; death of parents, 105; his views on religious freedom, 108-10; writes novel on religion, 109-10; is chancellor of the exchequer, 113, 115, 122, 127; is leader of House of Commons, 114-16; his relations with queen, 115, 130-32, 139-42, 176-79, 181; questions and bills he is interested in, 120-23, 127-28, 133-34; Napoleon among his friends, 124; death of sister Sarah, 128; is leader of the opposition, 128-30; hires private secretary, 132; is popular with people, 135, 146; receives honors,

135, 146; is appointed prime minister, 136; serves only nine months, 142-43; refuses title, 143-44; continues as opposition leader in Commons, 144; writes romantic satire, 144-45; is worried about Mary Anne, 145; his wife dies, 147; is prime minister again, 152; reforms passed by his government, 152-54; foreign affairs under him, 154-57, 166-74, 175-76; buys controlling interest in Suez Canal, 158-62; becomes ill, 165-66, 171; is given title, 168; receives Order of the Garter, 175; is no longer prime minister, 176; writes novel during illness, 179-80; his health failing, 180; death of, 181; his grave visited by queen, 182

D'Israeli, Isaac (father), 15-19, 20-25, 27-28, 30, 31-32, 43, 61-62, 63, 80, 104-05

Disraeli, James (brother), 18, 20, 30

D'Israeli, Maria (mother), 17, 18, 20, 24-25, 105

Disraeli, Mary Anne (wife), 77-80, 87, 89, 90, 97, 101, 105-06, 111, 119, 124, 130, 132, 134-35, 136-37, 141, 143, 144, 145, 146-50. *See also* Lewis, Mary Anne

Disraeli, Ralph (brother), 18, 20, 30

D'Israeli, Sarah (grandmother), 14-15

Disraeli, Sarah (sister), 18, 20, 30, 31, 44, 45, 51, 57, 63, 69, 86, 89, 115, 128

Don Quixote, 47

drainage system, bill for, 123

Durham, Lord, 56

East India Company, 122-23

Edinburgh, University of, 135

education bills, 76, 144

Edward I, 13

# INDEX

Whig party, 54, 56, 62, 64, 66, 68, 85-86, 101, 117, 128
Wight, Isle of, 176
William IV, 63
Willyams, Mrs. Brydges, 118-19
Windsor Castle, 130, 132
workhouses, 66, 83

Xaprut, Spanish House of, 14

*Young Duke,* 45
"Young England" group, 89-91, 98

Zulus, the, 176

## About the Author

MANUEL KOMROFF was born in New York City, and educated in schools there and at Yale. He worked as a newspaper man and during World War I as a war correspondent. His first short stories appeared in 1918, and since then one hundred and thirty of them have been published. He is also the author of many adult novels and biographies of famous historical personages for young people. For a number of years he lectured at Columbia University where he conducted a Novel Writing Workshop. He is a member of the Author's Guild, P.E.N., the Overseas Press Club.